Daily Inspiration
and
Encouragement
for Bikers

365 Verses
365 Prayers

Joel Tuminaro

Copyright © 2014 by Joel A. Tuminaro

ISBN: DROP ISBN-13 HERE

Edited by Sue Gaffield

Cover Design by Jim Lipiano
Lipiano Design, 2014

Printed in the United States of America

365 Verses 365 Prayers

Do you ever start your day with prayer and can't think of what to pray for? The first step is to read some Scripture. The second step is to pray for yourself, based on what you have just read. Often, we pray for our missionaries, our neighbors, the prayer requests of our congregation, but not specifically for our relationship with God. We may ask God to fulfill our needs and often our desires, but all of these things are temporary. When Jabez asked God to "Bless me indeed" (1 Chronicles 4:9-10) it wasn't just for physical blessings, more land, more money, more cattle, or overall prosperity. The Bible says that Jabez was "more honorable than his brethren". Jabez wanted a closer relationship with God.

Like Solomon, who asked for an "understanding heart" (1 Kings 3:9), what he was really asking for was wisdom. Solomon's desire was for wisdom to lead God's people, and Jabez wanted the wisdom just to please God.

By praying for themselves, these and other great men and women of faith became a spiritual blessing to all those around them and the physical blessings naturally followed. (Matthew 6: 33)

When you can't think of what to pray for, first start by praising God just for who He is. This is normal communication with your Creator and brings you into His presence (Psalm 22:3) whether you feel as if your specific needs are currently met or not. Secondly, you must spend time reading the Bible. <u>Prayer and Bible reading must go together.</u>

Presented in this book are daily Scriptures, each with a corresponding prayer. Here's an example:

You, my brothers, were called to be free. But do not use your freedom to indulge the sinful nature; rather, serve one another in love. The entire law is summed up in a single command: "Love your neighbor as yourself." Galatians 5:13-14

And the corresponding prayer:

God, I thank you today for freedom; the freedom to worship, the freedom from sin and the freedom to ride and serve with my brothers and sisters. Thank you for your great love. Help me to love my neighbor and honor you. Amen.

So having read a verse, you now have a prayer that goes along with it.

Many times we pray as a habit, about any issue, ignoring the Scripture we have just read. <u>Your daily Bible reading should generate a daily prayer!</u>

If you pray only when you need something, there's a good chance you're not spending enough time reading God's word. The Bible tells us what we need and therefore what we should pray for.

When scripture is put in, prayer naturally flows out. This book is by no means a substitute for daily Bible reading and prayer. Keep it on your desk at work or by your bed to start or finish your day. Use it as a daily reminder that there is an ever-increasing benefit from God's Word and from time spent alone with Him.

In 1604, King James I of England authorized that a new translation of the Bible into English be started. It was finished in 1611, just 85 years after the first translation of the New Testament into English appeared (Tyndale, 1526). The Authorized Version, or King James Version, quickly became the standard for English-speaking Protestants. Its flowing language and prose rhythm has had a profound influence on the literature of the past 300 years. The King James Version presented here is public domain in the United States.

JANUARY

"EVERY word of GOD is FLAWLESS;

he is a SHIELD to those who take REFUGE in HIM."

PROVERBS 30:5

JANUARY 1

My son, if you will receive my words, and hide my commandments with you; so that you incline your ear unto wisdom, and apply your heart to understanding; you cry after knowledge, and lift up your voice for understanding; If you seek her as silver, and search for her as for hidden treasures; shall you understand the fear of the LORD, and find the knowledge of God. For the LORD gives wisdom: out of his mouth come knowledge and understanding.   Proverbs 2:1-5.

Heavenly Father, walk with me today and guide my steps. Grant me insight and wisdom as I strive to serve you better each day. Increase my desire for your Word and help me to understand the fear of the Lord and attain the knowledge of God. In Jesus' name, Amen.

JANUARY 2

Trust in the Lord and do good; so shalt thou dwell in the land, and verily thou shalt be fed. Psalm 37:3.

Lord, grant me an opportunity to serve you and others today. I trust you in all that I do. Help me to trust you more. In Jesus' name, Amen.

JANUARY 3

He that hath my commandments, and keepeth them, he it is that loveth me: and he that loveth me shall be loved of my Father, and I will love him, and will manifest myself to him.   John 14:21

Lord, help me to love you more and more each day, for as my love for you increases, so will my obedience. Thank you for the love of God that reveals the heart of Jesus to mine, Amen.

JANUARY 4

Hast thou not known? hast thou not heard, that the everlasting God, the LORD, the Creator of the ends of the earth, fainteth not, neither is weary? there is no searching of his understanding.   Isaiah 40:28

Creator of all that exists, thank you that you are willing to meet me anytime, anyplace and hear my prayer. I may not understand all that is going on in my life, but today I choose to trust in your wisdom, Amen.

JANUARY 5

And this is the promise that he hath promised us, even eternal life.   1 John 2: 25

Lord, teach me to give priority to things that are eternal. Help me to let go of the temporary things of this world. Thank you Jesus, Amen.

JANUARY 6

For the wages of sin is death; but the gift of God is eternal life through Jesus Christ our Lord. Romans 6:23

Thank you God, for the free gift of eternal life through Jesus. Keep my mind focused on you so that I may be free from sin and death. In Jesus' name I pray, Amen.

JANUARY 7

Bless the LORD, O my soul: and all that is within me, bless his holy name.   Psalm 103:1

Heavenly Father, help me to lift up your name today, not just in words, but in all that I do. I bless your name today and every day, Amen.

JANUARY 8

A wholesome tongue is a tree of life: but perverseness therein is a breach in the spirit.
Proverbs 15:4

Dear God, help me in all that I say and do today to reflect the beauty of Christ. I pray that you would speak words of life and health through me. In Jesus' name, Amen.

JANUARY 9

Let every thing that hath breath praise the LORD. Praise ye the LORD.   Psalm 150:6

Lord, as I start my day, help me to praise you in all that I do. Help me to praise you for each person that I come in contact with and every blessing you lavish upon me and in every situation I confront. Help me to be in a spirit of praise all day so that I may feel your presence. Thank you Jesus, Amen.

JANUARY 10

Looking for that blessed hope, and the glorious appearing of the great God and our Saviour Jesus Christ; Who gave himself for us, that he might redeem us from all iniquity, and purify unto himself a peculiar people, zealous of good works.   Titus 2:13-14

Father, make me holy. Holy Spirit, draw me closer, Jesus, make me eager. Do these things for your praise and for the blessing of those who need to know you better. Please forgive me for the times I have settled for less in my Christian walk and stir me to a holy passion to serve you. In Jesus' name, Amen.

JANUARY 11

Now therefore ye are no more strangers and for-eigners, but fellow citizens with the saints, and of the household of God; And are built upon the foundation of the apostles and prophets, Jesus Christ himself being the chief corner stone.   Ephesians 2:19-20

Thank you Great God that I belong to God's people. Thank you for making me an important part of your house. Thank you that I can be a part of your promises, your grace, and your plan, Amen.

JANUARY 12

Let your face shine on your servant; save me in your unfailing love.   Psalm 31:16

Thank you for always being there, God. Deliver me today from things that might keep me from your presence, Amen.

Joel A. Tuminaro

JANUARY 13

For a day in thy courts is better than a thousand. I had rather be a doorkeeper in the house of my God, than to dwell in the tents of wickedness.   Psalm 84:10

Help me mighty God to walk in your courts today. Help me to desire your presence over the things of this world. In Jesus' name I pray, Amen.

JANUARY 14

So teach us to number our days, that we may apply our hearts unto wisdom.   Psalm 90:12

Holy and Almighty God, King of the Ages, you alone live in complete wisdom, justice, and grace. Please help me to know what time it is in my life and the role you want me to play at this stage of my journey. I want my life to be lived glorifying you. In Jesus' precious name I pray, Amen.

JANUARY 15

Stand up and bless the LORD your God for ever and ever: and blessed be thy glorious name, which is exalted above all blessing and praise.   Nehemiah 9:5

Heavenly Father, I don't understand the love that causes an eternal and mighty God to listen to my prayers. Yet I know you do hear them and respond to them. Thank you! Please be praised in my worship, whether I offer it in private, with other Christians at church, in my daily personal devotions, or in my public worship. Help me to be an example before my coworkers. You alone are God and worthy of all praise; please be praised in my life. In the name of Jesus I pray, Amen.

JANUARY 16

For we are but of yesterday, and know nothing, because our days upon earth are a shadow.   Job 8:9

Holy and Almighty God, thank you so much for your overwhelming patience as you try to communicate your love to people like me with my limited abilities to comprehend your glory. It's as if I was indeed born yesterday! Please give me wisdom today, to make the decisions I need to make and to choose your way and not my own. In the name of the Lord Jesus Christ I pray, Amen.

JANUARY 17

Call unto me, and I will answer thee, and show thee great and mighty things, which thou knowest not. Jeremiah 33:3

Awesome God, I want to know you and to be known by you. Thank you Lord that you answer when I call so that I can reflect your glory and display your character. Thank you for the gift of being your child and having my future secured. In Jesus' name, Amen.

JANUARY 18

Show me thy ways, O LORD; teach me thy paths. Lead me in thy truth, and teach me: for thou art the God of my salvation; on thee do I wait all the day. Psalm 25:4-5

O mighty God, please help me to know your will more completely. Help me to wait on you so I can live for you and to please you. I want others to know of my relationship with you – not just through the words I speak, but also through the character of my conduct. In Jesus' name I pray, Amen.

JANUARY 19

Charge them that are rich in this world, that they be not high minded, nor trust in uncertain riches, but in the living God, who giveth us richly all things to enjoy.   1 Timothy 6:17

Faithful and loving God, I thank you that you are the one in whom I can find my identity, hope and future. You have blessed me in so many ways. Help me work to put my trust in you and not in earthly wealth or possessions. I give you all glory and praise, now and forever. In the name of Jesus I pray, Amen.

JANUARY 20

But without faith it is impossible to please him: for he that cometh to God must believe that he is, and that he is a rewarder of them that diligently seek him. Hebrews 11:6

Holy God, I do seek to know you better. Help me to diligently do so each day. Please make your presence known more powerfully in my life and in the life of your Church. In Jesus' name I pray, Amen.

January 21

And that ye study to be quiet, and to do your own business, and to work with your own hands, as we commanded you; that ye may walk honestly toward them that are without, and that ye may have lack of nothing.   1 Thessalonians 4:11-12

Holy and righteous Father, I need your help to learn to slow down and tend to my own responsibilities instead of running around out of control and without purpose. Please grant me not only the wisdom that I have been praying for, but also the patience and calm that I need for that wisdom to change my heart and mind.   In Jesus' name I pray, Amen.

January 22

Yet a little while, and the world seeth me no more; but ye see me: because I live, ye shall live also. John 14:19

Thank you Lord for opening my spiritual eyes to see you, in the love of Christians, in nature and in your Holy Word. Thank you that because you live I can now have eternal life. Help me to walk in your path and be more like you! In your name I pray, Amen.

JANUARY 23

Where no wood is, there the fire goes out: so where there is no talebearer, strife ceases.
Proverbs 26:20

Forgive me, O God, for the times I have kept gossip alive or have entertained conversation of gossip. Please bless and heal those whom I have wounded with my participation in gossip. Give me the wisdom to say only what is helpful to others and blesses them. Help me to mend the relationships that I have damaged because of reckless words, and the wisdom to know how to discourage those who would spread gossip. In Jesus' name I pray, Amen.

JANUARY 24

For the LORD will not forsake his people for his great name's sake: because it hath pleased the LORD to make you his people.   1 Samuel 12:22

Holy and Righteous God, your grace has not only saved me, but sustains me even when my own failures can cause me to doubt. Thank you for loving me despite my unworthiness and giving me righteousness so that I will be fit for your kingdom and glory. In Jesus' name I praise you, Amen.

JANUARY 25

Be of the same mind one toward another. Mind not high things, but condescend to men of low estate. Be not wise in your own conceits.   Romans 12:16

Father, thank you for making me in your image, designed personally by you with a purpose that will bring you glory. Help me to not think too much of myself and my importance. Please help me to be around those with whom you want me to associate. In Jesus' name I pray, Amen.

JANUARY 26

Verily, verily, I say unto you, except a corn of wheat fall into the ground and die, it abides alone: but if it dies, it brings forth much fruit.   John 12:24

Help me today God to die to myself and to my own desires. Make me a reflection of you and your character so that I can blossom and grow in grace to bring forth fruit that glorifies you. In Jesus' name, Amen.

JANUARY 27

O worship the LORD in the beauty of holiness: fear before him, all the earth.   Psalm 96:9

You are holy, majestic God, more than my mind can grasp or my imagination can fathom. I worship and praise you for your glory, might, grace, and mercy. I look forward to the day when I can see your splendor face to face and join the angels of heaven in never ending worship and praise. Through Jesus I offer this praise and my life to you, Amen.

JANUARY 28

But whoso keeps his word, in him verily is the love of God perfected: hereby know we that we are in him. He that says he abides in Him ought himself also so to walk, even as He walked.   1 John 2:5-6

Stir my spirit, O God, and empower me with your Spirit to live a life of integrity and purity like Jesus. Please give me a heart for people, dear Father, like Jesus has. Help me to not just see their needs and hear their cries, but to also respond with love and compassion. In the name of my Savior Jesus, I pray, Amen.

JANUARY 29

Wine is a mocker, strong drink is raging: and whosoever is deceived thereby is not wise. Proverbs 20:1

Father, my heart hurts today for every person, and every family, caught under the influence of Satan because of alcohol and drug abuse. Please bless those who are burdened by a loved one in the grip of an addiction. May they receive from you the courage to seek help and not remain alone and silent. Please awaken their loved one to the truth of his/her destructive lifestyle. Please prepare the people who can guide them to the road to recovery, health, and freedom that you so long to give them. Please use us, your Church, as a place of healing and hope for those whose lives are caught in this terrible trap. In Jesus' name I pray for your mighty help and power, Amen.

JANUARY 30

Even from the days of your fathers you are gone away from my ordinances, and have not kept them. Return unto me, and I will return unto you, says the LORD of hosts.   Malachi 3:7

O God, please forgive me for seeking my own way. I confess that I have wandered from you. Even while the Bible is so readily available I often squander the opportunity to hear you speak from your Word. Even when there are so many opportunities to praise you and pray to you, you sometimes only hear from me when I have gotten myself into trouble. Father, I confess that I have let my relationship with you slip and that I have not pursued your presence in my life as much as I could. Please be with me and all your Church as we seek you and your presence daily in our lives! In Jesus' name I pray, Amen.

JANUARY **31**

For where two or three come together in my name, there am I with them.   Matthew 18:20

Father, thank you for sending your Son, not just to minister here while he walked the earth, but also to bless us with his presence during our worship. Open my heart to rejoice in his presence as I meet with friends who share my faith. In the name of the Lord Jesus I pray, Amen.

FEBRUARY

Give thanks to
the Lord, for he is
good; his love endures
forever.

psalm 106:1

FEBRUARY 1

Recompense to no man evil for evil. Provide things honest in the sight of all men.
Romans 12:17-18

Forgive me, O God, for the grudges I've held and the evil things I've thought about others. Help me to see and to value them as Jesus does. In your name I pray, Amen.

FEBRUARY 2

Looking unto Jesus the author and finisher of our faith; who for the joy that was set before him endured the cross, despising the shame, and is set down at the right hand of the throne of God.
 Hebrews 12:2

Holy God, forgive me when I chase what is false and let my focus shift from Jesus as my Savior. I want to honor and serve him, having his life come alive in me, so that others may know the confidence that comes from having Jesus as their Lord. Words cannot express my gratitude for his sacrifice and the price he paid for my sins or my thanks for his victory over sin and death that assures that I will some-day be with you forever! It is in the name of Jesus Christ that I pray, Amen.

FEBRUARY 3

Be kindly affectionate one to another with brotherly love; in honor preferring one another.
Romans 12:10

Dear God, my loving Father, thank you for surrounding me with so many godly and honorable people. Please help me find ways each day that I can show them my appreciation and love. In Jesus' name I pray, Amen.

FEBRUARY 4

Help us, O God of our salvation, for the glory of thy name: and deliver us, and purge away our sins, for thy name's sake.   Psalm 79:9

Holy and awesome God, I need your forgiveness and grace. I need your deliverance from the tempter's snare. Without your power and mercy, I will surely fail. May the grace you extend to me bring you glory. May the forgiveness you lavish upon me bring others to honor your name. In Jesus' name I pray, Amen.

FEBRUARY 5

But let all those that put their trust in thee rejoice: let them ever shout for joy, because thou defendest them: let them also that love thy name be joyful in thee.   Psalm 5:11

Mighty and awesome God, please bless us with peace. Grant us relief from the horrors the world has afflicted on your children through the hatred of men. Give us the courage, in good or bad times, to be open about our faith, generous with our forgiveness, and steadfast in prayer. In Jesus' name I pray, Amen.

FEBRUARY 6

Who hath delivered us from the power of darkness, and hath translated us into the kingdom of his dear Son.   Colossians 1:13

Heavenly Father, make us into a people of hope, love and of your character. Cast out all darkness from our hearts. Shine the light of your grace through us so people can see your children as a healing for the nations. In the name of the Lord Jesus Christ, the only true Savior of all people, I pray. Amen.

FEBRUARY 7

Whom having not seen, ye love; in whom, though now ye see him not, yet believing, ye rejoice with joy unspeakable and full of glory: Receiving the end of your faith, even the salvation of your souls.
1 Peter 1:8-9

What joy fills my heart, Father, when I think about what it will be like to be in your presence—to have you wipe each tear from my eyes and to have you introduce me again to those I love and to those great men and women of faith I've only known by reputation. Please never let me outlive that sense of anticipation and never let the hope of eternity with you dim in my heart, no matter what else may happen in my life here. In Jesus' name I pray, Amen.

FEBRUARY 8

Glory in his holy name; let the hearts of those who seek the LORD rejoice. 1 Chronicles 16:10

You have blessed me in so many ways, Father. How can I ever begin to thank you? I confess that I sometimes seek notoriety for myself even though I know it is only false flattery. But deep in my heart, dear God, I know that my true glory is found in the adoption covenant signed with Jesus' blood. Thank you! Words cannot express my gratitude, but please know that I look forward to being eternally grateful for all that you have done. May the glory be yours in heaven and earth, both now and forever. In the name of Jesus I praise you, Amen.

FEBRUARY 9

Thou, even thou, art LORD alone; thou hast made heaven, the heaven of heavens, with their entire host, the earth, and all things that are therein, the seas, and all that is therein, and thou preserve them all; and the host of heaven worship thee.
Nehemiah 9:6

Awesome God, you alone are Lord of all creation and the Lord of my life. All you have made and all of your works cry out and declare your creativity and your loving kindness. Father, I offer my praise to the chorus of creation, the voices of the angels, and the praise of many who have come before me. You are worthy to be praised. I give you my worship, my songs, my heart, and my life. In Jesus' name, Amen.

FEBRUARY 10

He shall cover thee with his feathers, and under his wings shalt thou trust: his truth shall be thy shield and buckler.   Psalm 91:4

Heavenly Father; there are no words to express my gratitude and praise for your deliverance from death. You are the God who was and is and is to come. You are my Abba Father, who has adopted me and made me your own. I place my trust, my hope, and future in you and I will not be afraid. I find my refuge under your wings! All praise to you in the name of Jesus, Amen.

FEBRUARY 11

Thus will I magnify myself, and sanctify myself; and I will be known in the eyes of many nations, and they shall know that I am the LORD.   Ezekiel 38:23

Father, as your finite and imperfect child, I do have a wholesome dread of displeasing you. We are mortal and frail in comparison to your glory. But I have confidence in my relationship with you through Jesus, and God I want to honor and bless your name in all that I do each day. In Jesus' name I pray, Amen.

FEBRUARY 12

For whosoever shall give you a cup of water to drink in my name, because ye belong to Christ, verily I say unto you, he shall not lose his reward.
Mark 9:41

Dear Heavenly Father, please use me this week to be a blessing to everyone I come in contact with. And this week, Lord, let me cross paths with someone who really needs your grace. Please give me discernment to see them when you bring them near. Give me courage to reach out and bless them. Keep them on my heart and help me to love and to pray for them. In Jesus' name I ask for your help and grace to use this opportunity for your glory, Amen.

FEBRUARY 13

And I thank Christ Jesus our Lord, who hath enabled me, for that he counted me faithful, putting me into the ministry.   1 Timothy 1:12

I praise your name, O God my Creator. Thank you for Jesus who has redeemed me, given me talents to use for your glory, strengthened me, led me, and empowered me to serve. May you be glorified in all that I say and do and even think. In Jesus' name, Amen.

FEBRUARY 14

Thus speaketh the LORD of hosts, saying, Execute true judgment, and show mercy and compassions every man to his brother: and oppress not the widow, nor the fatherless, the stranger, nor the poor; and let none of you imagine evil against his brother in your heart.   Zechariah 7:9-10

Loving Father, please forgive me for the times I've failed to show mercy and compassion to others or thought less than wholesome thoughts about those who are not as fortunate. When my response to others is not what it should be, or my heart does not reach out to them, please use your Spirit to convict me so that I might live by this scripture and glorify you. In Jesus' name I pray, Amen.

FEBRUARY 15

He that commits sin is of the devil; for the devil sinned from the beginning. For this purpose the Son of God was manifested, that he might destroy the works of the devil.   1 John 3:8

Almighty God, you are the only rightful Lord of my heart. I pledge my allegiance to you. Please help to lay aside my battle with sin and empower me to live for you with unchanging loyalty. In the name of my Savior Jesus I pray, Amen.

FEBRUARY 16

Thy testimonies are very sure: holiness becomes your house, O LORD, for ever.   Psalm 93:5

Holy God, as you are Holy, please make me holy and forgive my sin by your grace. Fill me with your Spirit and bring forth your fruit in my life so that it reflects your character. Give me a desire to know your will and to seek your truth and an understanding of your Word so I can apply it to my life. Mold and shape my life with you as its center. In Jesus' precious name I pray, Amen.

February 17

Blessed is the man that endureth temptation: for when he is tried, he shall receive the crown of life, which the Lord hath promised to them that love him. James 1:12

Gracious God, thank you for promising the crown of life to me. Empower me to stand firm and endure temptation through the power of your Holy Spirit. In Jesus' name I pray, Amen.

February 18

And the world passes away, and the lust thereof: but he that doeth the will of God abides for ever. 1 John 2:17

Dear God, please help me to be honest about what I pursue with my life. I want it to count for you. I want to make a difference for good. I ask that this desire would not be self-serving, but would truly be a life that impacts others for righteousness and brings you glory. Help me not to waste time chasing things that don't last and don't really matter. Grant me the wisdom to follow you and find your will rather than shallow desires. In Jesus' name I pray, Amen.

February 19

Be thou exalted, LORD, in thine own strength: so will we sing and praise thy power.   Psalm 21:13

Heavenly Father your name is exalted above all things. I commit myself to daily praise and thanksgiving for all that you have done, and all that you are going to do. To you, the only true God, the Alpha and Omega, I offer my songs of praise and worship. In the awesome name of Jesus, I pray, Amen.

February 20

But the Lord is faithful, who shall establish you, and keep you from evil.   2 Thessalonians 3:3

Almighty God, thank you for giving me victory over sin. Please strengthen me so that I can overcome temptation and resist the Evil One. O Lord, it is only you that I am dedicated to worship and obey. To you belongs all glory forever, and ever, in the name of Jesus I pray, Amen.

FEBRUARY 21

I am the LORD thy God, which have brought thee out of the land of Egypt, out of the house of bondage. Thou shalt have no other gods before me. Exodus 20:2-3

Mighty and awesome God, you are worthy of all praise. I recognize that you are holy and your children should be holy. Help me to obey your Word and seek your will. I want to serve you with my whole heart. Help me to offer my obedience as freely as your blessings have been poured out upon me. In Jesus' name I pray, Amen.

FEBRUARY 22

If we confess our sins, he is faithful and just to forgive us our sins, and to cleanse us from all unrighteousness.   1 John 1:9

Thank you so much God, for your forgiveness and cleansing of my heart. I am sorry for my weakness, my failure to take strength in you. I am sorry for the times I disappointed you. Thank you for welcoming me home to your presence and reminding me that I am your child. Please help me to move past my failures and to grow more fully into the holiness of Jesus, in whose name I pray, Amen.

FEBRUARY 23

For every one that asketh receiveth; and he that seeketh findeth; and to him that knocketh it shall be opened.   Luke 11:10

Heavenly Father, sacrificing your son Jesus for my sin is a debt I can never repay. Salvation through Jesus is too wonderful for words. The gift of your presence in me through your Holy Spirit empowers me. Thank you for the assurance that as I seek you, you hear me. In Jesus' name I thank and praise you, Amen.

FEBRUARY 24

God is our refuge and strength, a very present help in trouble.   Psalm 46:1.

God, you are my protector and my only hope. Thank you Lord, for saving me. I thank you for hearing me when I call. I thank you for blessings, guidance and protection. Stay close by as I face the challenges that come up in life. Enable me to grow and be an example to others when storms arise. In the name of Jesus, my Savior, I pray, Amen.

FEBRUARY 25

Thy word is true from the beginning: and every one of thy righteous judgments endureth for ever. Psalm 119:160

Heavenly Father, I pray that my life would reflect your character in holiness and righteousness. You are an eternal God and I want my life to reflect eternal things. Give me wisdom to see through the temporary distractions that take my focus off of you. Help me to live for things that will glorify you for eternity. In Jesus' name, Amen.

FEBRUARY 26

For the LORD is our judge, the LORD is our lawgiver, the LORD is our king; he will save us. Isaiah 33:22

Everlasting Father, thank you for guarding my life and soul in your very hands. I know you love me because you sent Jesus to die for my sins. I know you are not willing that any should be lost because of your great love and mercy. I willingly trust my life and soul and eternal future to you. In Jesus' name I pray, Amen.

FEBRUARY 27

Thus saith the LORD, thy Redeemer, the Holy One of Israel; I am the LORD thy God which teacheth thee to profit, which leadeth thee by the way that thou should go.   Isaiah 48:17

Eternal Father, guide my steps to the places where you would have me go, to the ministries that you want me to serve in or give to, and to the people you want me to encounter. Give me a heart to do your will and let me do all things for your glory. In Jesus' name, Amen.

FEBRUARY 28

And Jesus came and spake unto them, saying, All power is given unto me in heaven and in earth. Go ye therefore, and teach all nations, baptizing them in the name of the Father, and of the Son, and of the Holy Ghost: Teaching them to observe all things whatsoever I have commanded you: and, lo, I am with you always, even unto the end of the world.   Amen. Matthew 28:18-20

Mighty and awesome God, our source of hope, send your Holy Spirit to stir within me a strong desire to share your Good News with others. Urge me out of my comfort zone and into your wonderful grace so that I can help others come to know your love. In the saving name of Jesus I pray, Amen.

MARCH

"THIS IS MY SON,
WHOM I HAVE CHOSEN;

LISTEN TO HIM."
LUKE 9 : 3 5

MARCH 1

We then that are strong ought to bear the infirmities of the weak, and not to please ourselves. Romans 15:1

Comforting Shepherd, help me to be sensitive to those who need your strength in their daily struggles. Remind me to offer encouragement and a listening ear. Help me to take note of their needs as you would. Show them how patient you are as you reveal to them your holiness. Thank you, O God, for your help in this area of my heart as I try to be a blessing to others. In Jesus' name I pray, Amen.

MARCH 2

Do all things without murmurings and disputing: That ye may be blameless and harmless, the sons of God, without rebuke, in the midst of a crooked and perverse nation, among whom ye shine as lights in the world. Philippians 2:14-15

Mighty and awesome God, thank you for calling me to such a holy task as following you. I want to stand up against the darkness of the things around me. Please help me as I seek to live a holy life that has a redeeming influence on those around me who do not know Jesus. In your name I pray, Amen.

MARCH 3

This book of the law shall not depart out of thy mouth; but thou shall meditate therein day and night, that thou may observe to do according to all that is written therein: for then thou shall make thy way prosperous, and then thou shall have good success. Joshua 1:8

Precious Lord, thank you that true success comes only from you. Obedience to you and to your Word brings blessing to me and all who I come in contact with. Help me to be an example of your character and to strive to live according to your Word. In Jesus' name I pray, Amen.

MARCH 4

The LORD redeems the soul of his servants: and none of them that trust in him shall be desolate. Psalm 34:22

Creator of everything, I place all that I am and all that I have in your hands. Use me O God to bless others as I strive to be your obedient servant. I entrust my future to you alone. Thank you Jesus, Amen.

MARCH 5

Wherefore he saith, Awake thou that sleep, and arise from the dead, and Christ shall give thee light. Ephesians 5:14

Dear Lord, help me to place a high value on my relationship with you. I look to you for all things. Help me to trust you with all my heart and walk in your light. In Jesus' name, Amen.

MARCH 6

And let us not be weary in well doing: for in due season we shall reap, if we faint not.   Galatians 6:9

Thank you God for the people who work tirelessly for you with no thought of recognition or reward. Help me to be one of those people and to serve you joyfully. In Jesus' name, Amen.

MARCH 7

Then said Jesus to those Jews which believed on him, if ye continue in my word, then are ye my disciples indeed.   John 8:31

Lord, help me to truly become your disciple. May my love for you increase, and my desire for your Word become my daily delight. I praise you today Lord, Amen.

MARCH 8

Blessed are the peacemakers: for they shall be called the children of God.   Matthew 5:9

Heavenly Father, help me to be a peacemaker to every life I come in contact with. Help me to do that which is good and to pursue peace. Help me to walk with you as your child, Amen.

MARCH 9

Yea, though I walk through the valley of the shadow of death, I will fear no evil: for thou art with me; thy rod and thy staff they comfort me.
Psalm 23:4

O God you are my Shepherd who defends and comforts me. I look to you alone for protection. When storms arise, I take shelter under your wing. Thank you Lord, that I can run to you and be safe, Amen.

MARCH 10

God is with thee in all that thou doest.
Genesis 21:22

God, I thank you that you've brought me this far. Show me your will day by day, so I can remain on the path that you have prepared for me. I commit my life, my plans and each day to you Great and Mighty God, Amen.

MARCH 11

Fear thou not; for I am with thee: be not dismayed; for I am thy God: I will strengthen thee; yea, I will help thee; yea, I will uphold thee with the right hand of my righteousness.   Isaiah 41:10

Lord, when I am afraid, help me to rest in your care. When things don't go the way I want them to, help me to trust in your strength. When I need help to stand, guide me with your righteousness. In Jesus' name I pray, Amen.

MARCH 12

Humble yourselves in the sight of the Lord, and He shall lift you up.   James 4:10

Lord, help me to humble myself and to be honest with myself and others in acknowledging my need for spiritual help, moral guidance, and divine help from you. Help me to draw closer to you each day. In Jesus' name I pray, Amen.

MARCH 13

I will pour out my Spirit upon all flesh.
Acts 2:17

Lord, I ask that you pour out your Spirit in my life in a special way today. Change my attitude to reflect your character and help me to conduct myself in a way that glorifies you. In Jesus' name I pray, Amen.

MARCH 14

Let us therefore come boldly unto the throne of grace, that we may obtain mercy, and find grace to help in time of need.   Hebrews 4:16

Dear Heavenly Father, it is a privilege to talk one on one with the Creator of the universe. I open my heart and mind to you. Grant me your grace today and keep me in the center of your will. In Jesus' name, Amen.

MARCH 15

And we know that all things work together for good to them that love God, to them who are the called according to his purpose.   Romans 8:28

Thank you God, for the assurance that I am called to you by your Spirit. Thank you God, that it is for your purpose. Help me to love you more and more each day as your purpose unfolds in my life, Amen.

MARCH 16

Sing and rejoice, O daughter of Zion: for, lo, I come, and I will dwell in the midst of thee, saith the LORD.   Zechariah 2:10

Lord help me to begin this day and every day in worship and dependence upon you. May my life be an instrument of praise to you. Thank you Jesus, Amen.

MARCH 17

Blessed shalt thou be when thou comest in, and blessed shalt thou be when thou goest out. Deuteronomy 28:6

Lord, I am truly blessed today in so many ways! Let my life reflect the joy that is in my heart that only comes from knowing you. In all that I do, may your name be glorified, Amen.

MARCH 18

And he said unto me, It is done. I am Alpha and Omega, the beginning and the end. I will give unto him that is athirst of the fountain of the water of life freely. Revelation 21:6

Thank you Lord, for the blessing of your Spirit and for your holy presence. Fill me with your joy to overflowing so that you might be glorified and others will experience your love, Amen.

MARCH 19

But whoso hearkens unto me shall dwell safely, and shall be quiet from fear of evil.   Proverbs 1:33

Lord, I look to your wisdom for my security. In this world where people cannot always feel safe and secure, help me to live in a way that helps others to find security in you also. Thank you Lord, that today I dwell in safety. Help me to continue to seek your wisdom, Amen.

MARCH 20

Know therefore that the LORD thy God, he is God, the faithful God, which keepeth covenant and mercy with them that love him and keep his commandments to a thousand generations.
Deuteronomy 7:9

Thank you, Lord that you hear my prayer. Thank you for revealing yourself to me through your Word. As I get to know you better and better, help me to rejoice in each new day spent in your presence, Amen.

MARCH 21

For thou, Lord, art good, and ready to forgive; and plenteous in mercy unto all them that call upon thee.   Psalm 86:5

Mighty and awesome God, thank you for loving me and dying so that I might live. Teach me to be good as you are good, to forgive as you forgive, to be merciful as you are merciful, and to call upon your name every day. Thank you Jesus, Amen.

MARCH 22

Casting all your care upon him; for he careth for you.   1 Peter 5:7

Lord, help me to lay my burdens at your feet, trusting you alone for strength and wisdom. Thank you that I can be at peace in your presence. Thank you for your great love, Amen.

MARCH 23

But my God shall supply all your needs according to his riches in glory by Christ Jesus.
Philippians 4:19

Heavenly Father, my need will never begin to exhaust your resources. Thank you God, that you are my supplier. I trust you in all things, Lord. Help me to trust you more each day. In Jesus' name, Amen.

MARCH 24

I have set the LORD always before me: because he is at my right hand, I shall not be moved.
Psalm 16:8

Thank you great and mighty God that there is confidence in my walk with you, that doing the right thing is natural when you are beside me. Make me and mold me in your image today, Lord. Help me to stay close to you, Amen.

MARCH 25

And he said unto me, My grace is sufficient for thee: for my strength is made perfect in weakness. Most gladly therefore will I rather glory in my infirmities, that the power of Christ may rest upon me. 2 Corinthians 12:9

Lord help me to be aware of my limitations. I pray that you would help me to be willing and ready to ask for your help, your guidance, and your wisdom. In your name I pray, Amen.

MARCH 26

Come now, and let us reason together, saith the Lord: though your sins be as scarlet, they shall be as white as snow; though they be red like crimson, they shall be as wool.　Isaiah 1:18

Thank you, Lord, that even though I was born into sin you sent Jesus to take my place on the cross. Thank you for washing away all of my guilt with his blood. Please help me to walk worthy of his sacrifice, Amen.

MARCH 27

And he said, My presence shall go with thee, and I will give thee rest.   Exodus 33:14

God, even when storms are all around us, you are near. Thank you for peace and safety. Help me to be still today and to listen for your voice. I praise you Lord, Amen.

MARCH 28

Thou wilt show me the path of life: in thy presence is fullness of joy; at thy right hand there are pleasures for evermore.   Psalm 16:11

Thank you Lord, for your presence. Thank you for the joy that comes from knowing Jesus. Help me to walk closer with you each day. In your name I pray, Amen.

MARCH 29

Again I say unto you, That if two of you shall agree on earth as touching any thing that they shall ask, it shall be done for them of my Father which is in heaven.   Matthew 18:19

Heavenly Father, forgive me for the times when my faith is weak. Help me to grow in faith and then to show it through compassion. Thank you that you always hear me when I call on your name in faith. In Jesus' name, Amen.

MARCH 30

Because he hath set his love upon me, therefore will I deliver him: I will set him on high, because he hath known my name. Psalm 91:14

Help me to love you more each day, Lord. Thank you for your deliverance when difficult situations arise. Thank you for the assurance that you know my needs before I ask. Remind me Lord to always call on your name, Amen.

MARCH 31

And if thou draw out thy soul to the hungry, and satisfy the afflicted soul; then shall thy light rise in obscurity and thy darkness be as the noon day. Isaiah 58:10

Lord, help me to be aware of those around me in need. Use me to reach out to those who are in want and distress, to share with them your love and grace. In Jesus' name I pray, Amen.

APRIL

COME
TO ME, ALL
YOU WHO ARE
WEARY & BURDENED,
& I WILL GIVE YOU REST.

MATTHEW 11:28

April 1

For in the time of trouble he shall hide me in his pavilion: in the secret of his tabernacle shall he hide me; he shall set me up upon a rock.   Psalm 27:5

Thank you Lord that you have all the strength I need in times of trouble. Increase my faith in you as I learn to trust you more each day. Help me to recognize the areas where I need to grow. In Jesus' name, Amen.

April 2

My sheep hear my voice, and I know them, and they follow me: And I give unto them eternal life; and they shall never perish, neither shall any man pluck them out of my hand.   John 10:27,28

Thank you Lord that you hold me safe in your hand. Help me to find quiet time each day to spend alone with you. Please help me to always listen for and recognize your voice. I offer you my praises today and every day, Amen.

APRIL 3

And he said unto them, Follow me, and I will make you fishers of men.   Matthew 4:19

Mighty and awesome God, send laborers out into your harvest. Send me Lord, Amen.

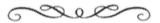

APRIL 4

Rejoice ye in that day, and leap for joy: for, behold, your reward is great in heaven: for in the like manner did their fathers unto the prophets. Luke 6:23

Lord, help me to live each day with joy. Let others see in me the joy that comes from knowing you. Put even more joy in my life as I draw closer to you, Lord, Amen.

APRIL 5

Blessed be the Lord, who daily loads us with benefits, even the God of our salvation.   Psalm 68:19

God of love, I do bless your name today. Thank you God, that you don't just give an occasional tiny blessing, but that you load us with awesome blessings every day. Help me to not take for granted all of the many blessings heaped upon my life every day. I can never thank you enough Lord, Amen.

APRIL 6

Then shalt thou call, and the LORD shall answer; thou shalt cry, and he shall say, Here I am. Isaiah 58:9

Lord I praise you that someone like me can enter into the courts of the King, no waiting, no special status, and you receive me as a friend everyday. Thank you God, for the privilege of prayer. Remind me to spend time with you each day, Amen.

APRIL 7

The eternal God is thy refuge, and underneath are the everlasting arms. Deuteronomy 33:27

God of love and protection, I give myself fully to you today Lord, only you dispel fear and anxiety. Remind me that I belong to you and that you are my safe haven. In Jesus' name I pray, Amen.

APRIL 8

I am come a light into the world, that whosoever believeth on me should not abide in darkness. John 12:46

Thank you Eternal God for sending your son into the world as the Light. Help me to walk in the Light so that all darkness is dispelled before me. Thank you God, for providing the path and for the Light to show the way, Amen.

APRIL 9

And whosoever shall give to drink unto one of these little ones a cup of cold water only in the name of a disciple, verily I say unto you, he shall in no wise lose his reward. Matthew 10:42

Lord, send someone my way today, someone who needs a smile, a hug, or a word of encouragement. Use me today great and loving God, to share the joy of knowing Jesus. Help me to bless someone who needs you, Amen.

APRIL 10

Commit thy way unto the LORD; trust also in him; and he shall bring it to pass. Psalm 37:5

Lord, today help me to strive to be more like you. Show me where change needs to occur, and help me to trust you to do the work in my life that will change me. I bless your name today God, Amen.

APRIL 11

And God is able to make all grace abound toward you; that ye, always having all sufficiency in all things, may abound to every good work. II Corinthians 9:8

Thank you God for the assurance that Jesus is mine and I am his. I place this day in your care. Help me to be open to your Spirit and leading, Amen.

APRIL 12

The LORD is nigh unto them that are of a broken heart; and saves such as be of a contrite spirit. Psalm 34:18

Thank you God, for your holy presence. Remind me to stay close to you all day. I praise you Lord, Amen.

April 13

Heaven and earth shall pass away: but my words shall not pass away. Luke 21:33

Lord, help me not to look aside to things that try to distract me from your Word and your Son, the only true way to salvation. Thank you Jesus, Amen.

April 14

God shall bless us; and all the ends of the earth shall fear him.   Psalm 67:7

Lord, your blessings are too many to count. Thank you that you demonstrate to the world every day how much you love me. Help me to walk in that great love today God, Amen.

APRIL 15

Ask, and it shall be given you; seek, and ye shall find; knock, and it shall be opened unto you. Matthew 7:7

God of every good thing, I thank you today for blessing every area of my life. In accordance with your holy Word, Lord, I ask you for more of your presence in my life, for the faith to trust you more, and for an opportunity to share your love with someone who is hurting and in need of you. Thank you most generous God, Amen.

APRIL 16

I will instruct thee and teach thee in the way which thou shalt go: I will guide thee with mine eye. Psalm 32:8

Lord, I am not worthy of all of the blessings you have lavished upon me. Thank you for your great love and mercy. Help me to trust you not just for daily needs but for guidance throughout my life. In Jesus' name I pray, Amen.

APRIL 17

Come unto me, all ye that labor and are heavy laden, and I will give you rest. Matthew 11:28

God you are the only God of comfort. I pray that when life brings up questions and worries that you would grant quiet and peace. I trust you for rest Lord, Amen.

APRIL 18

My help cometh from the LORD, which made heaven and earth. Psalm 121:2

Thank you Lord for sending the Holy Spirit who gives me power against temptation. Teach me O God to focus my mind on you and your great love, Amen.

APRIL 19

The fear of the LORD tendeth to life: and he that hath it shall abide satisfied; he shall not be visited with evil.   Proverbs 19:23

Thank you Lord, for being always near. Give me a wholesome fear of displeasing you. Help me to keep you always on my mind. Thank you for standing in between me and evil, Amen.

APRIL 20

For whosoever will save his life shall lose it; but whosoever shall lose his life for my sake and the gospel's, the same shall save it.   Mark 8:35

Lord you are a great and mighty God. Help me to do great and mighty things for you. In your name I pray, Amen.

April 21

I love them that love me; and those that seek me early shall find me.   Proverbs 8:17

Lord, help me to search your Word often for the wisdom that you provide. Thank you for sending the Holy Spirit to guide and direct my ways, Amen.

April 22

For verily I say unto you, Till heaven and earth pass, one jot or one tittle shall in no wise pass from the law, till all be fulfilled.   Matthew 5:18

Lord, you are the God who crosses every t and dots every i. Thank you Lord that even the smallest details cannot escape you. Thank you, faithful God that you are never too busy to remember all of your promises. In Jesus name, Amen.

April 23

And it shall come to pass, that before they call, I will answer; and while they are yet speaking, I will hear. Isaiah 65:24

Before I even begin to pray, Lord you answer me. Thank you Lord, that the solution to all of my questions and problems is already there. I simply have to trust you for the outcome. Help me to trust you more each day, Amen.

April 24

Set your affection on things above, not on things on the earth.   Colossians 3:2

Thank you God, that you have prepared a future that will erase all of the temporary things here on earth that don't matter. Help me to look forward to eternity with you and not get caught up in small distractions here. In Jesus' name I ask it, Amen.

APRIL **25**

Then spake Jesus again unto them, saying, I am the light of the world: he that followeth me shall not walk in darkness, but shall have the light of life. John 8:12

Help me to follow you, God. Help me to listen. Thank you for your Son Jesus who scatters all of the darkness. Help me to walk in the light of life,   Amen.

APRIL **26**

Judge not, and ye shall not be judged: condemn not, and ye shall not be condemned: forgive, and ye shall be forgiven. Luke 6:37

Lord please forgive me for the times I have stood in judgment of others. Since I desperately need your forgiveness, help me always to forgive. Thank you God, for this great promise, Amen.

APRIL 27

And call upon me in the day of trouble: I will deliver thee, and thou shalt glorify me.   Psalm 50:15

Heavenly Father, you promised wisdom to those who seek you. Help me to look to you first in all things. I give you all of the praise Lord. In Jesus' name, Amen.

APRIL 28

For I will pour water upon him that is thirsty, and floods upon the dry ground: I will pour my spirit upon thy seed, and my blessing upon thine offspring. Isaiah 44:3

Thank you God, that you are my source. You are not a stingy God. You didn't promise just a sip, but floods. You not only want to bless me, but my offspring as well. Thank you God, that I can seek you for all things, and you are faithful to answer, Amen.

APRIL **29**

The LORD knoweth the days of the upright: and their inheritance shall be for ever.   Psalm 37:18

Mighty God, help me to always do my best knowing that you are right beside me ready to help in any situation. Thank you for the assurance that you are always there, Amen.

APRIL **30**

He gives power to the faint; and to them that have no might he increases strength. Isaiah 40:29

Help me today God to walk in the courage of my faith. Help me to be bold in telling others about Jesus. Please help me to rely on you more and more each day in everything that I do. In Jesus' name, Amen.

MAY

Do not let this
Book of the Law
depart from your
mouth; meditate on
it day & Night...
Joshua 1:8

MAY 1

The eyes of the LORD are upon the righteous, and his ears are open unto their cry.   Psalm 34:15

You always hear me Lord.   You know everything about me and understand all the things that concern me. Thank you God that I can call upon you anytime.   You're always there and you always listen.   I bless your holy name today God, Amen.

MAY 2

For with God nothing shall be impossible. Luke 1:37

Lord, I thank you that you are the God of the impossible.   There is no problem you cannot handle, no obstacle you cannot overcome.   When I feel overwhelmed, help me to remember the God I serve and to remember your promises.   I bless your name today, O God, Amen.

MAY 3

Heaven and earth shall pass away, but my words shall not pass away. Matthew 24:35

Help me great and mighty God, to remember that the heavens and the earth were formed simply by the power of your spoken Word and one day I will awake in your likeness. Help me to always listen to your Word and obey, Amen.

MAY 4

The LORD shall open unto thee his good treasure, the heaven to give the rain unto thy land in his season, and to bless all the work of thine hand. Deuteronomy 28:12

In all that I do Lord, help me to work for you. Let people see that I worship a God that blesses everything that I touch, and who prospers all that I set out to accomplish for your glory. In Jesus' name I ask it, Amen.

MAY 5

The Lord knoweth how to deliver the godly out of temptations. 2 Peter 2:9

Lord I thank you for the ways you have delivered me from temptation in the past. Help me again today Lord to withstand any temptation that would keep me from knowing you better and from walking in your will. In Jesus' name I pray, Amen.

MAY 6

Blessed are they which are persecuted for righteousness' sake: for theirs is the kingdom of heaven. Matthew 5:10

Heavenly Father, help me to lift my eyes above the things around me that are disquieting. Please help me to focus my thoughts and my affections on you Most High God, Amen.

MAY 7

He that goeth forth and weepeth, bearing precious seed, shall doubtless come again with rejoicing,
bringing his sheaves with him.   Psalm 126:6

*Lord, help me not to give up too quickly on the peo-
ple that I am trying to influence in a Godly way. Remind
me often to pray for those who need you and to live my life
as an example. Thank you for saving me Lord, Amen.*

MAY 8

And I will establish my covenant with you, neither shall all flesh be cut off any more by the waters of
a flood; neither shall there any more be a flood to
destroy the earth.   Genesis 9:11

*Awesome God I pray that through you I would have
a life built upon a firm foundation. Help me to diligently
seek your guidance in all that I do. In Jesus' name I ask it,
Amen.*

May 9

And it shall come to pass, that whosoever shall call on the name of the Lord shall be saved. Acts 2:21

Thank you great God, for saving me from a life of disaster. Please help me to always walk in a manner worthy of being called a Christian, Amen.

May 10

The righteous cry, and the LORD heareth, and delivereth them out of all their troubles. Psalm 34:17

Thank you God for all of the wonderful things you have already done in my life. Help me to not be afraid to ask for help when I need it. Help me to lean on you even more, Amen.

MAY 11

Trust in the LORD with all thine heart; and lean not unto thine own understanding. In all thy ways acknowledge him, and he shall direct thy paths. Proverbs 3:5-6

I trust you Lord; help me to trust you more. May I realize that your plan is best for me even when I don't understand some of the things going on around me. I acknowledge you as Lord of my life and trust you to direct me. Thank you, Lord, Amen.

MAY 12

But the word of the Lord endureth for ever. And this is the word which by the gospel is preached unto you. 1 Peter 1:25

God, sometimes my mind cannot always grasp a clear understanding of your eternal Word. I believe that it is inspired of the Holy Spirit and speaks to me of your nature and your character. Please help me to listen to you and know you better each day through your Word, Amen.

May 13

But he that shall endure unto the end, the same shall be saved. Matthew 24:13

Precious Lord Jesus, give me a faith that does not waiver. Help me to trust you implicitly and seek your guidance in all things. In your name I ask it, Amen.

May 14

Cast thy burden upon the Lord, and he shall sustain thee: he shall never suffer the righteous to be moved. Psalm 55:22

My trust is in you Lord. I pray that I would never give in to discouragement. Stay present in my thoughts each day. Help me to seek your wisdom in all things, Amen.

MAY 15

As the Father hath loved me, so have I loved you: continue ye in my love. John 15:9

I love you Lord, because you first loved me. Even when I was dirty and undeserving, you loved me with unchangeable love. Help me to walk in that love every day of my life, Amen.

MAY 16

For the people shall dwell in Zion at Jerusalem: thou shalt weep no more: he will be very gracious unto thee at the voice of thy cry; when he shall hear it, he will answer thee. Isaiah 30:19

Lord, I pray that you would help me to always remember that what you have spoken you will do. Thank you Lord, for the confidence that I can fully trust your Word, Amen

MAY 17

Many are the afflictions of the righteous: but the LORD delivereth him out of them all. Psalm 34:19

Lord I know there are times when you have to discipline your child. Help me to understand the reasons for your chastening. Teach me to be more like you Lord. Amen.

MAY 18

The meek will he guide in judgment: and the meek will he teach his way. Psalm 25:9

Most Holy God, when I have failed because of a lack of faith or a lack of wisdom, help me to step aside and allow you to work in my life. Please help me to rely more upon your unfailing power and love. In Jesus' name, Amen.

MAY 19

Rejoice not against me, O mine enemy: when I fall, I shall arise; when I sit in darkness, the Lord shall be a light unto me.   Micah 7:8

Thank you so much God for providing a Light in such a dark world. Keep my mind focused upon you that I may continue to walk in that Light, Amen.

MAY 20

The LORD is my strength and song, and he is become my salvation. Exodus 15:2

Mighty and awesome God, I ask that you direct each step I take today Lord. Help me to take my strength from you alone when a crisis arises or someone reaches out to me for help. Thank you for always being there,   Amen.

MAY 21

Behold, I stand at the door, and knock: if any man hear my voice, and open the door, I will come in to him, and will sup with him, and he with me. Revelation 3:20

Lord you are always knocking. Help me to be still today and listen for your gentle call. Help me to wait in your presence and be sensitive to your voice. In Jesus' name, Amen.

MAY 22

Draw nigh to God, and he will draw nigh to you. James 4:8

Thank you Lord, for your promises. If I reach out, you respond. May I reach out to you more and more, Amen.

MAY 23

The LORD will perfect that which concerneth me: thy mercy, O LORD, endureth for ever.
Psalm 138:8

Thank you Lord that true joy comes from knowing you. Thank you for the peace that comes from knowing that all that concerns me is in your hands today. Thank you for your great love and mercy. I love you too, Lord, Amen.

MAY 24

Therefore if any man be in Christ, he is a new creature: old things are passed away; behold, all things are become new. 2 Corinthians 5:17

Thank you Lord for the change that has come over me. Thank you for washing me with your blood. Help me to resist the temptations that tug me in the wrong direction as I walk in newness of life. In your precious name I pray, Amen.

May 25

But as truly as I live, all the earth shall be filled with the glory of the Lord. Numbers 14:21

Lord there are countless reminders of your good-ness, your creativity, your power and your majesty. I praise you for being such an awesome God. Be glorified in my life today, Lord. In your name I ask it, Amen.

May 26

For the Lord shall be thine everlasting light, and the days of thy mourning shall be ended. Isaiah 60:20

Prince of Peace, thank you for the comfort of your Holy Spirit. Thank you for always being there and drying every tear. I praise you today Lord, Amen.

MAY 27

All that the Father giveth me shall come to me; and him that cometh to me I will in no wise cast out. John 6:37

Lord I am the object of your constant love and affection. Remind me today, Lord to walk in that love and to share it with others. Thank you that you hear all who cry out to you. I bless your holy name today God, Amen.

MAY 28

For thou, LORD, wilt bless the righteous; with favor wilt thou compass him as with a shield. Psalm 5:12

Help me to be righteous in your sight God. I want to receive your blessing today. Thank you for your eternal presence and loving protection that surrounds me, Amen.

MAY 29

He that overcometh shall inherit all things; and I will be his God, and he shall be my son. Revelation 21:7

Lord today I ask that you cleanse me of all impurities. Help me to overcome all of the things around me that try to distract me from being your child. In Jesus' name, Amen.

MAY 30

I am the door: by me if any man enters in, he shall be saved, and shall go in and out, and find pasture. John 10:9

Thank you, Lord, for being the Way. Thank you for showing me the door that pardons me from a sentence of death. Thank you, Lord, for the freedom that comes from being your child. I love you Lord, Amen.

MAY 31

Wait on the LORD: be of good courage, and he shall strengthen thine heart: wait, I say, on the LORD. Psalm 27:14

Lord I confess I get confused sometimes and walk around in fear not knowing what to do. Please help me to listen for your voice and wait for guidance from you. I trust you for all of the answers Lord, Amen.

JUNE

The good man brings
good things out of
the good stored up
in his heart...

Luke 6:45

JUNE 1

Wherefore we receiving a kingdom which cannot be moved, let us have grace, whereby we may serve God acceptably with reverence and godly fear. Hebrews 12:28

King of kings I praise you and thank you for giving me a position in your unconquerable kingdom. In Jesus' name I praise you, Amen.

JUNE 2

Now ye are the body of Christ, and members in particular. 1 Corinthians 12:27

Father, thank you for making me a part of something so awesome, as the body of Christ. Please help each person in my church family to find his or her gifts of ministry and to use those gifts in ways that touch others with your heart and that bring you glory. In Jesus' name, Amen.

JUNE 3

But thou shalt remember the LORD thy God: for it is he that giveth thee power to get wealth, that he may establish his covenant which he swore unto thy fathers, as it is this day.   Deuteronomy 8:18

God you are so generous and I know I don't deserve all of the blessings you lavish upon me. Forgive me for the times I've acted like I earned it all. Jesus did deserve it all and yet gave it all up for me. Thank you for your mercy, your grace, for salvation and all of the other blessings in my life. In Jesus' name I thank you, Amen.

JUNE 4

God thunders marvelously with his voice; great things does he, which we cannot comprehend. Job 37:5

Mighty and awesome God of the thunder, the moun-tains, the endless night with countless stars, the crashing ocean teeming with life, the earth rich with its animals, birds and insects, I praise you that you cared enough to make even me with unique fingerprints. You even know my name and the number of hairs on my head! I will never comprehend your glory Lord, but I ask that you help me walk in your grace. In Jesus' name I pray, Amen.

JUNE 5

In all these things we are more than conquerors through him who loved us.   Romans 8:37

Awesome God, Jesus' victory over death is my victory, too. Please make me a living testimony to your power, mercy, and grace. In Jesus' name, and for his glory, I live and pray, Amen.

JUNE 6

Rejoice in the LORD, ye righteous; and give thanks at the remembrance of his holiness.
Psalm 97:12

Holy and loving God, I thank you Lord for who you are. You are far greater than my mind can understand and more generous than I can ever deserve. So I offer you my thanksgiving and praise, and I pray that my life reflects my appreciation for all that you are and all that you have done for me. I bless your name today Lord, Amen.

JUNE 7

I will praise the name of God with a song, and will magnify him with thanksgiving. Psalm 69:30

Lord I offer you my praise today. Please forgive me for waiting for a holiday to acknowledge your glory. All of nature reflects your generosity, kindness and creativity. I can never count all of the reasons to praise you. As you continue to bless us with your Holy Spirit, may you fill our mouths with songs of praise and let everyday be a day set aside to praise you. In Jesus' holy name I pray, Amen.

JUNE 8

And they that be wise shall shine as the brightness of the firmament; and they that turn many to righteousness as the stars for ever and ever. Daniel 12:3

God, today I ask a special blessing on all who minister in your name. I pray for those who are forced to worship in secret and those who are persecuted for your name's sake. Bless all who strive to further your kingdom. May their lives be a reflection of your glory as they carry your Holy Word to a world stained with sin. In Jesus' name I pray, Amen.

JUNE 9

To the only wise God be glory forever through Jesus Christ! Amen. Romans 16:27

Awesome God, I pray that you would be glorified in the lives of your people. May we always sing your praises and declare your glory. I pray that others would see your love on our faces and hear it in our worship. Use me and other believers to influence those around us who need Jesus. In your majestic name I pray, Amen.

JUNE 10

O satisfy us early with thy mercy; that we may rejoice and be glad all our days. Psalm 90:14

Great and glorious God, fill my heart with your Holy Spirit today so that your love and joy overflow. Fill me with an abiding sense of your presence. In the name of Jesus I pray, Amen.

June 11

For he hath made him to be sin for us, who knew no sin; that we might be made the righteousness of God in him. 2 Corinthians 5:21

Thank you, loving Father, for saving me. Thank you for sending your son to die in my place. I pray that my life would be a testimony of your mercy and your grace. Shine through me today, Lord, so that others who don't know you would see your love. In Jesus' name, Amen.

June 12

But let the righteous be glad; let them rejoice before God: yea, let them exceedingly rejoice. Psalm 68:3

God, I pray that you would help me to be more thankful and to spend more time in worship and in praise of your awesome works. Please be with those who are persecuted for loving you and send peace where there is hardship and victory where there is no freedom. Help me always to rejoice for the new life I enjoy because of being in relationship with you. May all of your children offer you highest praise! Amen.

JUNE 13

And beside this, giving all diligence, add to your faith virtue; and to virtue knowledge; And to knowledge temperance; and to temperance patience; and to patience godliness; And to godliness brotherly kindness; and to brotherly kindness charity. For if these things be in you, and abound, they make you that ye shall neither be barren nor unfruitful in the knowledge of our Lord Jesus Christ.   2 Peter 1:5-8

Lord, in obedience to your Word, help me to be more and more like you each day. Use me to share all of these Godly traits with those I come in contact with so that they will know I belong to you. Help me to grow in the knowledge of your grace and character. In Jesus' name I pray, Amen.

JUNE 14

But if we walk in the light, as he is in the light, we have fellowship one with another, and the blood of Jesus Christ his Son cleanseth us from all sin. 1 John 1:7

Wonderful God, help me to honor Jesus and his death on the cross by living a pure and holy life. Thank you for leading me to other believers who could tell me about you. Thank you for making me into a new creature. Give me a greater desire for your Word and for worship with other believers. In Jesus' name, Amen.

JUNE 15

My son, if sinners entice thee, consent thou not. Proverbs 1:10

Lord, I thank you that when I am faced with temptation you always provide a way of escape. Please help me to walk in integrity. Let my life be an example of one who was transformed by the blood of Jesus. Help me to protect and guide others who may be tempted. In Your name I pray, Amen.

JUNE 16

And rend your heart, and not your garments, and turn unto the LORD your God: for he is gracious and merciful, slow to anger, and of great kindness, and repenteth him of the evil. Joel 2:13

Dear God, when I am tempted to sin, please help me to be sensitive to the Holy Spirit and pay attention to my conscience. Help me to have a broken heart over displeasing you. Help me not to take for granted the extreme sacrifice you paid for my sin. Please keep my heart pure so I can serve you better. In Jesus' name, Amen.

June 17

Then I said unto you, Dread not, neither be afraid of them. The LORD your God which goeth before you, he shall fight for you, according to all that he did for you in Egypt before your eyes. Deuteronomy 1:29-30

Lord, I praise you today for all you have done to bless, save and redeem your people. Give me an increase in faith to expect great things from you. Give me an open heart to hear and obey your Word, and a mind and will to tell others about you. In your name I pray, Amen.

June 18

My little children, these things write I unto you, that ye sin not. And if any man sin, we have an advocate with the Father, Jesus Christ the righteous: And he is the propitiation for our sins: and not for ours only, but also for the sins of the whole world. 1 John 2:1-2

Father, I'm ashamed at my weakness when I sin. In those moments of shame, help me to be more aware that Jesus provided the way back into your presence. Jesus, I thank you for coming to my rescue. Please help me not to get discouraged when I fall. Instead, I re-commit myself to live in a manner that honors you and for your glory. In the name of Jesus, my Lord, I pray, Amen.

June 19

Let nothing be done through strife or vainglory; but in lowliness of mind let each esteem other better than themselves. Philippians 2:3

Almighty God, thank you for adopting me as your child and making me pure and of value to your kingdom. Please help me to see myself as I really am in relation to you, like a little tiny grain of sand standing beside a mighty mountain. Please give me a servant's heart so that others can see your glory. In Jesus' name I pray, Amen.

June 20

But God, who is rich in mercy, for his great love wherewith he loved us, Even when we were dead in sins, hath quickened us together with Christ, (by grace ye are saved;). Ephesians 2:4-5

Mighty and awesome God, how can I ever praise you enough for your infinite love and great mercy? Thank you God that you did all of this for your good purpose and that you have planned no defeat for your people. Thank you for changing my life God, Amen.

JUNE 21

As ye have therefore received Christ Jesus the Lord, so walk ye in him: Rooted and built up in him, and established in the faith, as ye have been taught, abounding therein with thanksgiving. Colossians 2:6-7

Holy and Righteous God, please help me to recognize sin and to avoid the situations and places where it's easy to get caught up in evil. I ask you for the wisdom to know what teaching lines up with your Word and what does not. Help me to live a holy life filled with thanksgiving that honors you, Amen.

JUNE 22

For we are his workmanship, created in Christ Jesus unto good works, which God hath before ordained that we should walk in them.
Ephesians 2:10

Thank you God for re-building me as your child. Thank you that you have ordained a right way of living. Thank you for the examples in your Word of what true obedience is. Please remind me today of how to act as a child of the King. In Jesus' name I pray, Amen.

JUNE 23

For the grace of God that brings salvation hath appeared to all men, teaching us that, denying ungodliness and worldly lusts, we should live soberly, righteously, and godly, in this present world. Titus 2:11-12

Heavenly Father, I praise you for your grace and love demonstrated to me by Jesus through his death and resurrection. Please give me the strength to walk away when faced with temptation. Help me to have a lifestyle that reflects your character and to walk worthy of your sacrifice. In Jesus' name I pray, Amen.

JUNE 24

Likewise the Spirit also helps our infirmities: for we know not what we should pray for as we ought: but the Spirit itself makes intercession for us with groaning which cannot be uttered. Romans 8:26

Lord Jesus, sometimes I don't know exactly how to pray as I should. Thank you Lord, that you know me better than I could ever know myself, and you know exactly what I need better than I know how to pray for it. Give me the confidence to know that even when my words fail, that you have my best interests at heart. I trust you in all things Lord, Amen.

June 25

And not only they, but ourselves also, which have the first fruits of the Spirit, even we ourselves groan within ourselves, waiting for the adoption, to wit, the redemption of our body. Romans 8:23

Holy God, you have blessed me in more ways than I can count. Thank you for giving me a new life here on earth. Even still, Lord, I long to be with you. I am frail and vulnerable in so many ways and look forward to that day when you take me home to be with you and make me perfect. Until that day, help me to be holy as you are holy, Amen.

June 26

For the earnest expectation of the creature waits for the manifestation of the sons of God. Romans 8:19

God of all creation you are the only hope of redemption. I long for the day that every tear is dried and my bondage to this temporary life is done. Please keep my mind set on the glory that will be revealed when Jesus comes back. In your name I pray, Amen.

June 27

For I reckon that the sufferings of this present time are not worthy to be compared with the glory which shall be revealed in us. Romans 8:18

Lord, when things are difficult, help me to trust you even more. When it seems as though the struggle is too much to bear, help me to compare it to the glory that will be revealed when Jesus returns. Thank you Lord for a hope, a trust, and a confidence that only comes from you. In Jesus' name I ask it, Amen.

June 28

For ye have not received the spirit of bondage again to fear; but ye have received the Spirit of adoption, whereby we cry, Abba, Father. The Spirit itself bears witness with our spirit, that we are the children of God: Romans 8:15-16

God of my Help and Protection, thank you that you are always near. Thank you that I can approach your throne with confidence. Thank you God, that you have adopted me as your child. Thank you God, that there is no fear in you. Stay present in my mind today Lord and walk with me every moment as I strive to be more like you, Amen.

June 29

For if we have been planted together in the likeness of his death, we shall be also in the likeness of his resurrection: Knowing this, that our old man is crucified with him, that the body of sin might be destroyed, that henceforth we should not serve sin. Romans 6:5-6

Thank you mighty and awesome God, that there is no obligation to my old life. Thank you that all my sin was washed away by your blood. Help me to continue to walk in the freedom of your light, free from my old nature. Fill me with Your Spirit so that I might have an even stronger resistance to sin. In Your name I ask it, Amen.

June 30

For sin shall not have dominion over you: for ye are not under the law, but under grace. Romans 6:14

Lord Jesus, as I fill my mind and heart with your Word each day, let the Light that fills my life dispel the darkness that once ruled me. Help me to be open and receptive to your grace and dead to all sin. In Jesus' name I pray, Amen.

JULY

"My sheep hear my voice. I know them, and they follow me."

John 10:27

July 1

For verily I say unto you, If ye have faith as a grain of mustard seed, ye shall say unto this mountain, Remove hence to yonder place; and it shall remove; and nothing shall be impossible unto you. Matthew 17:20

Thank you God, that the same power that raised Jesus from the dead is available to me. Please increase my level of faith so that I can serve you better each day. When doubt creeps in Lord, help me to remember that it's your power I rely on, not mine, Amen.

July 2

And as ye would that men should do to you, do ye also to them likewise. Luke 6:31

Dear God, there are times that I am not treated as I feel I should be. Please help me to always return good to each person that I come in contact with so that your name will be glorified. I pray that my conduct will reflect the beauty of Christ. In His name I ask it, Amen.

JULY 3

And above all things have fervent charity among yourselves: for charity shall cover the multitude of sins. 1 Peter 4:8

Loving and gracious Father, help me to love my neighbor today Lord. I know that if I truly love others, then I will act in a manner that will show people that I belong to you. I pray that you send me an opportunity to show someone an act of kindness today. In your name and for your glory I pray, Amen.

JULY 4

But whosoever drinketh of the water that I shall give him shall never thirst; but the water that I shall give him shall be in him a well of water springing up into everlasting life. John 4:14

Thank you God, for the fountain of eternal life that you provide in response to a world being born into sin and death. Thank you Lord, that because of Jesus I will never thirst again. I praise you today Lord, for everlasting life through him, Amen.

July 5

Bear ye one another's burdens, and so fulfill the law of Christ. Galatians 6:2

Help me to raise up a brother or a sister who has fallen Lord. Build in me a holy compassion that I would seek to bear the burden of someone who needs a special touch from you. Help me to remember to pray for those in need, and to bless all those you send my way, in Jesus' name, Amen.

July 6

Greater love hath no man than this, than a man lay down his life for his friends. John 15:13

Heavenly Father, I can see in your Word that the emphasis is not just on "friends" but on the laying down of a life, because Jesus didn't just die for his friends, but also for his enemies. I realize that I could never live up to the love of Christ. It is only through your grace that I am saved. Thank you for your great mercy and love. Help me to ponder it all day today and begin to scratch the surface of who you are, Amen.

July 7

Bless them which persecute you: bless, and curse not. Romans 12:14

Mighty God, It's hard for me to empathize with brothers and sisters who are forced to worship you in secret. I have so much freedom that I take for granted that I can worship you anytime and anywhere. I pray today Father for those who are persecuted for your holy name. I pray that you would give them peace in their trials, victory over oppression and a holy love for those who seek to stand between them and you. I ask a special blessing upon those who would persecute Christians. Touch their hearts Lord and show them your amazing grace. In Jesus' name I pray, Amen.

July 8

And now abides faith, hope, charity, these three; but the greatest of these is charity.
1 Corinthians 13:13

Send someone across my path today Lord Jesus, someone who needs a hug, a kind word or deed or just someone to listen. Help me to share with others the greatest Love in the world, Amen.

July 9

And also that every man should eat and drink, and enjoy the good of all his labor, it is the gift of God. Ecclesiastes 3:13

Thank you Great and Mighty God. It is truly through you that I can labor and have enough food and drink to satisfy me. Help me to remember those who may not have enough work to sustain them. Please help me to be a blessing to those who are struggling to find work and feed their families. In Jesus' name, Amen.

July 10

Thou hast turned for me my mourning into dancing: thou hast put off my sackcloth, and girded me with gladness; to the end that my glory may sing praise to thee, and not be silent. O LORD my God, I will give thanks unto thee for ever. Psalm 30:11-12

Forgive me Lord for the times I have failed to acknowledge that you are the source of all of the good things in my life. I can never sing enough praises to your holy name. Lord, even when everything is in my favor, let me not forget to call upon your name. Let me put my trust in you and you alone. In Jesus' name I pray, Amen.

July 11

Fight the good fight of faith, lay hold on eternal life, whereunto thou art also called, and hast professed a good profession before many witnesses. 1Timothy 6:12

Lord, when it feels as if my Christian life becomes a struggle, remind me that the world is watching and I must take my strength from you to fight corruption, temptation, and the powers of darkness that would try to keep me from you. In Jesus name I ask it, Amen

July 12

Know ye not that ye are the temple of God, and that the Spirit of God dwells in you?
1 Corinthians 3:16

Lord I ask today that you help me to discipline myself and to care for this temple and keep it holy. Help me to not be lazy in exercise, and to never be abusive or harmful to my body. Thank you for my body God. I offer it to you as a clean and healthy place to live. In Jesus' name, Amen

July 13

Blessed be the name of God for ever and ever: for wisdom and might are his. Daniel 2:20

Lord just as Daniel sought to hear from you about the king's dream, I covet the prayers of other Christians. I am the most blessed when others seek your face on my behalf. Thank you Lord that you grant wisdom if we would but ask. Thank you for those who pray for me. Help me to remember others in prayer too, Amen.

July 14

The name of the LORD is a strong tower: the righteous run to it, and are safe.   Proverbs 18:10

Thank you God, that I can take rest in you when I am weary and take sanctuary in you when I am pursued. Keep my conscience strong Lord, and help me to remain righteous in your sight so that I can run to you and be safe. I praise you today for being my refuge, Amen.

July 15

The LORD is my strength and my shield; my heart trusted in him, and I am helped: therefore my heart greatly rejoices; and with my song will I praise him.   Psalm 28:7

Thank you Lord, that you have heard my cry. You have been my strength and my shield in both the good times and the bad. Help me to praise you by living my life in a way that honors you, Amen.

July 16

Be strong and of a good courage, fear not, nor be afraid of them: for the LORD thy God, he it is that doth go with thee; he will not fail thee, nor forsake thee. Deuteronomy 31:6

Heavenly Father, it is comforting to know that you are right beside me even in the middle of a great storm. When people turn against me, you never fail. When situations arise that are not meant for my good, you are right there every step of the way. I thank you for your presence in my life Lord. When troubles arise, help me to remember that you are never far away.   In Jesus' name I pray, Amen.

JULY 17

But when they saw him walking upon the sea, they supposed it had been a spirit, and cried out: For they all saw him, and were troubled. And immediately he talked with them, and said unto them, be of good cheer: it is I; be not afraid. And he went up unto them into the ship; and the wind ceased: and they were sore amazed in themselves beyond measure, and wondered. Mark 6:49-51

God I confess that sometimes I feel like I'm tossed around on an angry sea. Please help me to focus my eyes and heart on you and not on the wind and the waves. Lord, you silenced the fears of the disciples by making yourself known to them. Make yourself known to me too, Lord, so that no trial can hinder your presence. Thank you for the peace that comes from knowing you, Amen.

JULY 18

But sanctify the Lord God in your hearts: and be ready always to give an answer to every man that asketh you a reason of the hope that is in you with meekness and fear: 1 Peter 3:15

Lord you may not have chosen me to be a great speaker, and you don't need me to defend you, but I pray that you would help me to sanctify you before others so that I live in a manner that encourages others to glorify and reverence you. When the time comes, please help me to acknowledge and explain my relationship with you with meekness and fear of God and not of man, Amen.

July **19**

The LORD liveth; and blessed be my rock; and let the God of my salvation be exalted. Psalm 18:46

Lord, you are the same God that raised Lazarus from the dead, the same Jesus that turned water into wine, and the same Holy Spirit that inspired your Holy Word. I praise you that you live today! Be exalted in my life. In Jesus' name I pray, Amen

July **20**

And their sins and iniquities will I remember no more. Hebrews 10:17

Mighty and awesome God I thank and praise you today that you are the God of forgiveness and that you not only cover my sins, but never bring them up again. Thank you for not requiring sacrifices or rituals to earn forgiveness. I only have to ask. Thank you God, Amen.

July 21

Commit thy works unto the LORD, and thy thoughts shall be established. Proverbs 16:3

Heavenly Father, pride, ignorance and self indulgence can make my plans turn into trouble. I pray that you would guide my thoughts and help me plan things for myself that will glorify you. I commit all of my plans and desires to you. Establish my thoughts today Lord, Amen.

July 22

For if ye forgive men their trespasses, your heavenly Father will also forgive you.   Matthew 6:14

God of forgiveness, I pray that you would help me not only to reconcile to you, but to others as well as a way to show your love. Help me to have a merciful and forgiving spirit just as you have had with me. In Jesus' name, Amen.

July 23

The LORD is my light and my salvation; whom shall I fear? the LORD is the strength of my life; of whom shall I be afraid? Psalm 27:1

Lord because of your presence, power and promises you are my light and my salvation. Because of your open ear to my every prayer, you are the strength of my life. Thank you that I can walk without fear, Amen.

July 24

Beloved, if God so loved us, we ought also to love one another.   1 John 4:11

God of Love, help me to see the image of you in your people. You are love and because I am your child I pray that I would reflect Godly Love to every person I come in contact with. In Jesus' name, Amen.

July 25

As far as the east is from the west, so far hath he removed our transgressions from us.
Psalm 103:12

Creator of Heaven and Earth, I know there is a North and there is a South, so there is a North Pole and a South Pole. We can see these places on a map. But God if you go from the East to the West, you just keep going around and around forever, and never get there. It's a place you can never find, so I thank you and praise you God, that it is to this place that is at a distance of "forever" that you have sent my sin. Help me to keep it there by living in a way that honors you. In Jesus' name I ask it, Amen.

July 26

There is therefore now no condemnation to them which are in Christ Jesus, who walk not after the flesh, but after the Spirit. Romans 8:1

Thank you Lord that I am chastened, but not condemned. Lord, keeping outward laws is not enough. Help me to have inward obedience also, Amen.

July 27

Finally, be strong in the Lord and in his mighty power. Ephesians 6:1

Lord God Almighty, my Father and Shepherd, strengthen me with your might and grace today so that I can withstand the attacks and temptations of sin. In Jesus' name I ask it, Amen.

July 28

Dear children, let us stop just saying we love each other; let us really show it by our actions. 1 John 3:18

Lord of Love, send the Holy Spirit into my life to plant your love. Help me not just to love others because they love me or because it's easy. Help me to love the unlovable, the ones who have no one else to love them, and the ones who still have not experienced your awesome grace. Thank you for your infinite love God, Amen.

July 29

Anyone who listens to my teaching and obeys me is wise, like a person who builds a house on solid rock. Though the rain comes in torrents and the floodwaters rise and the winds beat against that house, it won't collapse, because it is built on rock. Matthew 7:24-25

Lord I know it's not enough just to acknowledge that you exist. Please help me to build my life upon the solid foundation of Jesus. Help me not to just have an outward profession of religion, but an inner relationship with you. When the storms come, I know that you will not be moved. Thank you, Jesus, for the firm foundation that keeps every-thing else in my life stable, Amen.

July 30

Take no part in the worthless deeds of evil and darkness; instead, rebuke and expose them. Ephesians 5:11

Great and mighty God, when there is evil all around me, help me to not only avoid it, but to reprove it and speak out for what is right. I pray that the light of Jesus would expose anything in my life that is not pleasing to you O God, Amen.

July 31

Let no corrupt communication proceed out of your mouth, but that which is good to the use of edifying, that it may minister grace unto the hearers. Ephesians 4:29

Lord, foul or abusive language won't just corrupt me; it damages all who have to hear it. Please remind me before I even open my mouth that every word that comes out should be helpful and encouraging. In Jesus' name I pray, Amen.

AUGUST

But the earth will
    be filled with the
    knowledge

of the glory
    of the Lord, as
        the waters
    cover the sea.

Habakkuk 2:14

AUGUST 1

Speaking to yourselves in psalms and hymns and spiritual songs, singing and making melody in your heart to the Lord; Giving thanks always for all things unto God and the Father in the name of our Lord Jesus Christ. Ephesians 5:19-20

My Lord and my God, you are awesome and wonderful. Your works are glorious and your deeds are beyond understanding. May the words of my mouth and the expressions of my heart always declare your praise. My heart is filled with thanksgiving for all that you have done to save me from sin, shame, and death. You are worthy of my praise, my songs, and my service. In the holy name of Jesus I pray, Amen.

AUGUST 2

All scripture is given by inspiration of God, and is profitable for doctrine, for reproof, for correction, for instruction in righteousness: That the man of God may be perfect, thoroughly furnished unto all good works.   2 Timothy 3:16-17

Lord it is an incredible gift that you would speak to me through your Word in my own language in a way that I can understand. Help me to study and search your Word for a deeper understanding of you. Let me never take for granted the awesome gift of being able to read your Word and learn more about you each day.   Please give me the character and the courage to put it into practice every day and use it to conduct my life in a way that honors you. In Jesus' name I pray, Amen.

August 3

Be sober, be vigilant; because your adversary the devil, as a roaring lion, walketh about, seeking whom he may devour: Whom resist steadfast in the faith, knowing that the same afflictions are accomplished in your brethren that are in the world. 1 Peter 5:8-9

Thank you, Most High God, for sending Jesus to lead me to victory over sin. I pray for protection from the things of the world that would seek to ensnare me. I thank you Lord that when the devil harasses me it is a sign of your favor, not your displeasure, just like with Job. And as you were with Job and delivered and blessed him, be with me too and deliver and bless me today, Lord. In the name of Jesus I pray, Amen.

August 4

The eyes of your understanding being enlightened; that ye may know what is the hope of his calling, and what is the riches of the glory of his inheritance in the saints. Ephesians 1:18

God of all creation, through the power of your Holy Spirit, please open my eyes of understanding. Help me to have a fuller understanding of your calling. Thank you Lord for the hope of eternal life through your son Jesus. In his name I pray, Amen.

AUGUST 5

For by grace are ye saved through faith; and that not of yourselves: it is the gift of God: Not of works, lest any man should boast.   Ephesians 2:8-9

Mighty and awesome God, thank you for sending Jesus to die on the cross for my sins. Help me to never take such an amazing gift lightly. Lord, help me to fully understand that salvation comes - not from me being good - but from your grace. Because you care so much about me, I pray that you would empower me to live a life that honors you. In the name of Jesus I ask it, Amen.

AUGUST 6

Let every soul be subject unto the higher powers. For there is no power but of God: the powers that be are ordained of God. Romans 13:1

King of kings and Lord of lords, there are no powers in existence except those you have allowed. You are the source of all authority. You have appointed governments and allowed them to be in place for the benefit of man. Lord I accept this as your divine arrangement. Lord, there are many instances where man has stepped in and corrupted what you have established. I ask a special blessing today, God, for those who are persecuted for your name. In places where people do not have the freedom of openly worshipping you, grant relief from oppression and true freedom that only comes from knowing you. In Jesus' name I pray, Amen.

AUGUST 7

But ye are a chosen generation, a royal priesthood, an holy nation, a peculiar people; that ye should show forth the praises of him who hath called you out of darkness into his marvelous light. 1 Peter 2:9

Great and Mighty God, I praise you and thank you for adopting me into your family. Please empower me Lord, to share your Good News with others so they might truly know that Jesus is Lord. In the name of my Savior, Jesus, I pray, Amen.

AUGUST 8

For this cause pay ye tribute also: for they are God's ministers, attending continually upon this very thing. Render therefore to all their dues: tribute to whom tribute is due; custom to whom custom; fear to whom fear; honor to whom honor. Romans 13:6-7

Sovereign God, I pledge allegiance to you. You alone are Holy. Heavenly Father, you have called me to honor my government, and you have blessed me to be in this country and have bestowed your grace upon me. I pray that you would empower me to live my life in a way that honors you and shows respect for my citizenship, and respect for all those I come in contact with. In Jesus' name I pray, Amen.

August 9

And if it seem evil unto you to serve the LORD, choose you this day whom ye will serve; whether the gods which your fathers served that were on the other side of the flood, or the gods of the Amorites, in whose land ye dwell: but as for me and my house, we will serve the LORD. Joshua 24:15

Lord, I pray that my house would be known as a place where the Most High God lives and is always welcome. Please help me to be a witness to my family, my friends, my co-workers and all who know me. Let my home life reflect the beauty of Christ, Amen.

August 10

Having made known unto us the mystery of his will, according to his good pleasure which he hath purposed in himself: That in the dispensation of the fullness of times he might gather together in one all things in Christ, both which are in heaven, and which are on earth; even in him. Ephesians 1:9-10

Thank you God, for revealing your plan for us through Jesus. Lord, I pray that every area of my life would be in submission to your will. For any area in my life that is not fully under your control, I ask that you send the Holy Spirit to convict and direct me to be totally in your will. In Jesus' name I ask it, Amen.

August 11

Who also hath made us able ministers of the new testament; not of the letter, but of the spirit: for the letter killeth, but the spirit giveth life. 2 Corinthians 3:6

Thank you Loving God, that we are under the ministry of grace; a New Covenant, not a written promise, but a spiritual one. What was written by man does not lead to life, but your Holy Spirit leads to eternal life through Jesus. Help me to learn your Gospel with all of my heart and also to share it, Amen.

August 12

I exhort therefore, that, first of all, supplications, prayers, intercessions, and giving of thanks, be made for all men; For kings, and for all that are in authority; that we may lead a quiet and peaceable life in all godliness and honesty.   1 Timothy 2:1-2

Awesome God, you have planned for me Godliness, honesty, integrity and dignity. You have also rightly planned that I intercede on behalf of the leaders you have put in authority. Please help me to love my pastor and my president, my boss and all other leaders who make vital decisions and to lift them up in prayer. Help me to focus on your will, not about what is less than perfect about leadership. Grant my leaders a special blessing today Lord, Amen.

AUGUST 13

Love not the world, neither the things that are in the world. If any man loves the world, the love of the Father is not in him. For all that is in the world, the lust of the flesh, and the lust of the eyes, and the pride of life, is not of the Father, but is of the world. 1 John 2:15-16

God of Love, I praise you that you are the provider of wisdom. Father, today I ask you for the wisdom to keep my attention on things that honor you, and not to be distracted by temporary things of this world. Fill me with a Godly love, so that my desire will be after things that are holy. In Jesus' name, Amen.

AUGUST 14

For so is the will of God, that with well doing ye may put to silence the ignorance of foolish men: As free, and not using your liberty for a cloak of maliciousness, but as the servants of God.
1 Peter 2:15-16

God, I represent you, so please give me the discipline to always do the right thing, so no one can speak poorly of me. Help me to use the freedom you have given me not to live any way that I want, but to live for you. In Jesus' name, Amen.

AUGUST 15

For Christ also hath once suffered for sins, the just for the unjust, that he might bring us to God, being put to death in the flesh, but quickened by the Spirit. 1 Peter 3:18

Amazing God, you traded the innocent for the condemned, so that you could draw me to yourself. Jesus was put to death in a mortal body, but brought to life by the Holy Spirit. Thank you God that I have a renewed life by that very same Spirit. Thank you for a changed life, Amen.

AUGUST 16

For this cause we also, since the day we heard it, do not cease to pray for you, and to desire that ye might be filled with the knowledge of his will in all wisdom and spiritual understanding. Colossians 1:9

Precious and Holy Father, today I pray for the Christians around the world who love and obey you. Though we all have different needs, the greatest need is to know you and to make you known. Please fill all of us with the knowledge of your grace through the Holy Spirit. Help us to honor you, reverence you and serve you until you take us home, Amen.

AUGUST 17

Sanctify them through thy truth: thy word is truth. John 17:17

Almighty God, things that are holy are dedicated to you and to you alone. Help me to be holy Lord, as you are holy. Please help me to saturate my mind with the knowledge of your Word and be more like you. In Jesus' name I ask it, Amen

AUGUST 18

Blessed is the man that walketh not in the counsel of the ungodly, nor standeth in the way of sinners, nor sitteth in the seat of the scornful. But his delight is in the law of the LORD; and in his law doth he meditate day and night.   Psalm 1:1-2

Lord, please give me more desire for your Word. Help me to manage my time and make you my priority. In Jesus' name I pray, Amen.

AUGUST 19

And how shall they preach, except they be sent? as it is written, How beautiful are the feet of them that preach the gospel of peace, and bring glad tidings of good things! Romans 10:15

Holy God, you are the God of all nations, yet so many have never even heard your name. Give me beautiful feet, Lord that I may be your missionary, whether it is across the world, across the country, across town, across the street or across the lunch table. Use me for your glory Lord, Amen.

AUGUST 20

Praise ye the LORD. Praise the LORD, O my soul. While I live will I praise the LORD: I will sing praises unto my God while I have any being.   Psalm 146:1-2

Thank you for these 2 simple, yet special verses Lord. Help me to repeat them all day long. In Jesus' name I pray, Amen.

AUGUST 21

I will praise thee, O LORD, among the people: and I will sing praises unto thee among the nations. Psalm 108:3

Righteous God, thank you for the songs that we sing in your praise. Thank you that inspiration comes from your Holy Spirit, not just to write lyrics and music, but to offer praises to your holy name. I ask for your blessings as I praise you Lord, not just by myself, but when I lift my voice with my church family as we worship you together. In Jesus' name, Amen.

AUGUST 22

Bless the LORD, O my soul, and forget not all his benefits: Who forgiveth all thine iniquities; who healeth all thy diseases; Psalm 103:2-3

Lord, you have made me clean inside, and have granted me health. Thank you God for restoring me to your favor and lavishing so many blessings upon me, Amen.

AUGUST 23

Thou hast seen it; for thou beholdest mischief and spite, to requite it with thy hand: the poor committeth himself unto thee; thou art the helper of the fatherless.   Psalm 10:14

You know the sorrow and the grief Lord, and hold it all in your hand. God as I pray for less fortunate people, stir in my heart a desire to reach out and help them, and to share Jesus, and to offer compassion and Godly love to a world that needs you. In Jesus' name I pray, Amen.

AUGUST 24

Arise, O LORD; O God, lift up thine hand: forget not the humble. Psalm 10:12

Lord bring a renewed desire for you back to our churches, restore our families and return our culture back to yourself in a time when so many are desperate for a healing that can only come from you. In Jesus' name, Amen.

AUGUST 25

A wicked man hardens his face: but as for the upright, he directs his way.   Proverbs 21:29

Lord forgive me for the times I have tried to hide my sin from others and from you. Help me to walk uprightly in your sight and to be an example to others. Help me to not be defiant, but to seek your face for guidance every day, Amen.

AUGUST 26

Bring forth therefore fruits worthy of repentance. Luke 3:8

Thank you for saving me from my sin, God. Please help me to dedicate my life to serving you. Give me the strength of your Holy Spirit to resist temptation and be more like you. In Jesus' name I ask it, Amen.

AUGUST 27

Pure religion and undefiled before God and the Father is this, to visit the fatherless and widows in their affliction, and to keep himself unspotted from the world.   James 1:27

Lord help me not only to remember in prayer the children who have no fathers or the widows who are in trouble, but to be stirred into action to help provide, to witness to, and to love those whom others may have forgotten, in Jesus' name, Amen

AUGUST 28

If any man among you seem to be religious, and bridleth not his tongue, but deceiveth his own heart, this man's religion is vain.   James 1:26

Loving and patient God, please forgive me for the times I have said things that do not honor you. Please let my speech be a blessing to others so that they can see you in my life. Let me be a reflection of your holy character Lord. In Jesus' name, Amen.

August 29

Cast away from you all your transgressions, whereby ye have transgressed; and make you a new heart and a new spirit: for why will ye die, O house of Israel? For I have no pleasure in the death of him that dieth, saith the Lord GOD: wherefore turn yourselves, and live ye. Ezekiel 18:31-32.

Lord I am unable to forsake the sin in my life until my heart is changed. I know that you are not willing that I should die, but you want to grant me eternal life. The change in my heart and in my life can only come from you, Mighty and Awesome God. By the grace of God, I will live only for you O Lord, Amen.

August 30

Then they that gladly received his word were baptized: and the same day there were added unto them about three thousand souls.   Acts 2:41

Most High God, send your Holy Spirit today to bring revival to our churches and salvation to many thousands who are lost in their sins. I ask this in Jesus' name, Amen.

AUGUST 31

And that from a child thou hast known the holy scriptures, which are able to make thee wise unto salvation through faith which is in Christ Jesus. 2 Timothy 3:15

Awesome God, your holy Scriptures give the knowledge and wisdom we need for salvation through Jesus Christ. Thank you God for familiar verses that are an inspiration to me. Help me to love your Word more and to absorb it everyday of my life, Amen.

SEPTEMBER

BUT THE FRUIT OF THE
SPIRIT IS LOVE, JOY,
PEACE, PATIENCE,
KINDNESS, GOODNESS,
FAITHFULNESS, GENTLENESS
AND SELF-CONTROL.

GALATIANS 5:22-23

SEPTEMBER 1

And Jesus said unto them, I am the bread of life: he that cometh to me shall never hunger; and he that believeth on me shall never thirst.   John 6:35

Lord, please help me to exercise my faith continually and come to you for what my soul craves. Thank you for being our eternal supply, Amen.

SEPTEMBER 2

· Him that overcometh will I make a pillar in the temple of my God, and he shall go no more out: and I will write upon him the name of my God, and the name of the city of my God, which is new Jerusalem, which cometh down out of heaven from my God: and I will write upon him my new name. Revelation 3:12

Gracious Heavenly Father, by the grace of God, I will overcome through Jesus. I thank you God that you have victory planned as the outcome for your people. Help me to stay worthy of bearing the name of the Most High God, Amen.

SEPTEMBER 3

For the LORD God is a sun and shield: the LORD will give grace and glory: no good thing will he withhold from them that walk uprightly.   Psalm 84:11

Mighty and Awesome God, your Spirit enlightens and comforts your people. You are a shield that protects us from all enemies. It is my greatest honor to have the favor of God upon me. Help me to walk uprightly O God so that you will withhold nothing from me. In Jesus' name, Amen

SEPTEMBER 4

In my Father's house are many mansions: if it were not so, I would have told you. I go to prepare a place for you.   John 14:2

Thank you holy God that you made room enough for all, even for me. Thank you God that knowing this eases a troubled mind, and calms my fears and reminds me that all I see here is temporary. Thank you God, for a mansion that will last forever, Amen.

Joel A. Tuminaro

SEPTEMBER 5

Blessed are they that mourn: for they shall be comforted.   Matthew 5:4

Dear Lord, help me to mourn for my sins and for the sins of others. Thank you Father, for a Godly sorrow that works true repentance. Help me to seek out your Holy Spirit to cleanse me, and help me to quietly submit to you, Amen.

SEPTEMBER 6

And the LORD said unto Joshua, This day will I begin to magnify thee in the sight of all Israel, that they may know that, as I was with Moses, so I will be with thee.   Joshua 3:7

Lord God Almighty, you blessed and encouraged Joshua, but you had even bigger things prepared for him. Your divine favor was upon him because he was on your mission. You are the powerful God that splashes oceans in two and that same power starts and completes our salvation. Help me to be on a mission for you God, and be with me as you were with Joshua, and with Moses. In Jesus' name I pray, Amen.

SEPTEMBER 7

The LORD is thy keeper: the LORD is thy shade upon thy right hand. Psalm 121:5

Lord, help me to always rely upon you alone and not on any man or earthly means. Holy Spirit you are my protector and comforter, abide with me forever. My confidence is in no one but you Lord. I bless your name today, Amen.

SEPTEMBER 8

A faithful man shall abound with blessings: but he that maketh haste to be rich shall not be innocent. Proverbs 28:20

God please keep my conscience strong so that I am faithful and upright in every transaction. Thank you God, that you honor me with blessings when I am faithful and honest. Help me to pursue integrity and not money. By the grace of God I will reflect the character of Jesus, Amen.

SEPTEMBER 9

The LORD bless thee, and keep thee: The LORD make his face shine upon thee, and be gracious unto thee: The LORD lift up his countenance upon thee, and give thee peace. Numbers 6:24-26

Thank you Lord, for Spiritual as well as earthly blessings. Thank you for saving me and keeping me, Great God. Thank you for forgiving my sin and supplying all my needs, and thank you for watching over me each day and granting me your peace, Amen.

SEPTEMBER 10

Thou art my hiding place; thou shalt preserve me from trouble; thou shalt compass me about with songs of deliverance. Selah. Psalm 32:7

Thank you Lord, that I can run to you and be safe. I praise you for keeping me out of trouble. May others around me see my deliverance and sing songs of praise to your holy name, Amen.

SEPTEMBER 11

Whither shall I go from thy spirit? or whither shall I flee from thy presence? If I ascend up into heaven, thou art there: if I make my bed in hell, behold, thou art there. If I take the wings of the morning, and dwell in the uttermost parts of the sea; even there shall thy hand lead me, and thy right hand shall hold me. Psalm 139:7-10

Even if I wanted to go out of your reach God, I can never be hidden from you. Thank you God for being near. Thank you for leading me. I trust you with all my heart, Amen.

SEPTEMBER 12

Thou hast also given me the shield of thy salvation: and thy right hand hath held me up, and thy gentleness hath made me great. Psalm 18:35

You have conquered every enemy God. You are my strength and my salvation. I can call on you for every trouble. I praise you for every time you have delivered me. Help me to always walk beside you, holy, and free from all sin. In Jesus' name I ask it, Amen.

SEPTEMBER 13

The fear of the wicked, it shall come upon him: but the desire of the righteous shall be granted. Proverbs 10:24

Thank you Jesus that through the power of the Holy Spirit, we can be righteous. Please help me to always have righteous thoughts and desires that are pleasing to you Lord, Amen.

SEPTEMBER 14

He healeth the broken in heart, and bindeth up their wounds. Psalm 147:3

Thank you Great and Mighty God for condescending to a broken hearted sinner like me to offer your love and healing. I praise you today for your great mercy, Amen.

SEPTEMBER 15

In whom we have boldness and access with confidence by the faith of him.   Ephesians 3:12

*Thank you God, that you grant the freedom to come
before your throne with bold confidence through faith in
Jesus Christ. Please help me to increase my faith and confidence in you. In Jesus' name I pray, Amen.*

SEPTEMBER 16

Which is come unto you, as it is in all the world;
and bringeth forth fruit, as it doth also in you, since
the day ye heard of it, and knew the grace of God in
truth.   Colossians 1:6

*Heavenly Father, the power of your Word produces
fruit wherever it is preached. Help me to carry your truth
with me wherever I go. In Jesus' name I pray, Amen.*

SEPTEMBER 17

And Thomas answered and said unto him, My LORD and my God. Jesus saith unto him, Thomas, because thou hast seen me, thou hast believed: blessed are they that have not seen, and yet have believed.   John 20:28-29

My Lord and my God, without faith I would be without Christ, without hope, without grace and without joy. Increase my faith today Lord, and if by that I should do great things, let me do them for you.   In faith I ask it, Amen.

SEPTEMBER 18

It is vain for you to rise up early, to sit up late, to eat the bread of sorrows: for so he giveth his beloved sleep.   Psalm 127:2

God I depend upon your blessing today, whether at rest, at work or traveling. Whatever success comes my way, I give you the glory, the honor and the praise, Amen.

SEPTEMBER 19

If the Son therefore shall make you free, ye shall be free indeed. John 8:36

Thank you Prince of Peace, for setting me free from the bondage of sin, Amen

SEPTEMBER 20

Then shall thy light break forth as the morning, and thine health shall spring forth speedily: and thy righteousness shall go before thee; the glory of the LORD shall be thy reward. Isaiah 58:8

Lord I acknowledge that all prosperity and health come from you. Help me to remember those less fortunate and to share not just food or shelter, but the love of Jesus, Amen.

SEPTEMBER 21

For I know the thoughts that I think toward you, saith the LORD, thoughts of peace, and not of evil, to give you an expected end. Jeremiah 29:11

Thank you Awesome God that you plan only good things for me, and have mapped out victory for my life. Thank you for answered prayers and a hopeful future, Amen.

SEPTEMBER 22

And when ye see this, your heart shall rejoice, and your bones shall flourish like an herb: and the hand of the LORD shall be known toward his servants, and his indignation toward his enemies. Isaiah 66:14

The joy of the Lord is my strength. I take comfort in you Lord. Thank you for revealing yourself to me God. I praise you for your mercy and for your justice, Amen.

SEPTEMBER 23

Confess your faults one to another, and pray one for another, that ye may be healed. The effectual fervent prayer of a righteous man availeth much. James 5:16

Thank you Jesus, for other Christians who pray for me, and who will listen, intending my highest good. Help me to be faithful in praying for them as well. In Jesus' name I pray, Amen.

SEPTEMBER 24

Now he that ministereth seed to the sower both minister bread for your food, and multiply your seed sown, and increase the fruits of your righteousness. 2 Corinthians 9:10

Creator of Heaven and earth, it is you that supplies the opportunity and the ability to help and serve others. Thank you God, that you richly bless me when I give. Help me always to represent you in my giving, Lord. In Jesus' name I pray, Amen.

SEPTEMBER 25

And of his fullness have all we received, and grace for grace.   For the law was given by Moses, but grace and truth came by Jesus Christ. John 1:16-17

Your blessings are too many to count Lord. Thank you Jesus for your immeasurable grace and love, Amen.

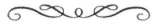

SEPTEMBER 26

The LORD shall preserve thee from all evil: he shall preserve thy soul. The LORD shall preserve thy going out and thy coming in from this time forth, and even for evermore.   Psalm 121:7-8

Lord I put no confidence in any hiding place but you and in no strength but yours. I trust you to keep me safe today Lord. In Jesus' name, Amen.

SEPTEMBER 27

And I have put my words in thy mouth, and I have covered thee in the shadow of mine hand, that I may plant the heavens, and lay the foundations of the earth, and say unto Zion, Thou art my people.
Isaiah 51:16

Thank you for watching over me today, Lord. Fill my mouth with your praises this day and every day, Amen.

SEPTEMBER 28

Better it is to be of an humble spirit with the lowly, than to divide the spoil with the proud. Proverbs 16:19

Help me to humble myself before you great and mighty God, and not to fear men but to fear pride in myself. Draw me closer to you today, Jesus. In your name I pray, Amen.

SEPTEMBER 29

What then? shall we sin, because we are not under the law, but under grace? God forbid.
Romans 6:15

Thank you for the deliverance that only comes from you, Lord. Thank you God, that we are not only free from the punishment of sin, but from being slaves to sin. Please help me to walk in your grace Jesus, Amen.

SEPTEMBER 30

Blessed be the God and Father of our Lord Jesus Christ, who hath blessed us with all spiritual blessings in heavenly places in Christ.   Ephesians 1:3

Lord I bless your name today for all of the rich blessings you have lavished upon me. Thank you God for the Spiritual blessings you give on earth that will be completed in heaven. Thank you God, that we can be with you forever. I praise you today and every day, Amen.

OCTOBER

I, am the vine; you are the branches.

John 15:5

OCTOBER 1

Blessed are the poor in spirit: for theirs is the kingdom of heaven.   Matthew 5:3

Lord, some happiness can come from earthly things, but blessedness comes from you. Thank you God, that a broken and contrite spirit brings blessedness, a much greater gift than happiness which is temporary. Help me to humble myself before you Lord, Amen.

OCTOBER 2

Delight thyself also in the LORD: and he shall give thee the desires of thine heart.   Psalm 37:4

Heavenly Father, to delight in you is as much a privilege as it is a duty. I thank you Lord, that my life does not depend upon abundance, but on all that you supply. Show me ways to delight myself in you today, Amen.

OCTOBER 3

Bless the LORD, O my soul, and forget not all his benefits: Psalm 103:2

Lord, King David sang this Psalm in recognition of your forgiveness, healing, rescue from hell, loving-kindness, compassion, blessings and restoration of youth. Thank you Great and Mighty God, that these same benefits are for me too through Jesus. I will bless your name today and every day, Amen.

OCTOBER 4

If any of you lack wisdom, let him ask of God, that giveth to all men liberally, and upbraideth not; and it shall be given him. James 1:5

I ask you for wisdom today God, so that I can serve you better. Thank you Lord, that if I use Godly wisdom all of your other blessings will follow. Increase my faith Lord, so that I will have all the wisdom I need to do your perfect will. In Jesus' name I pray, Amen.

OCTOBER 5

Blessed are the meek: for they shall inherit the earth.   Matthew 5:5

Help me to humble myself O God, to be mild and gentle, a good representative of you. Thank you for your blessings Lord, Amen.

OCTOBER 6

Wherefore he is able also to save them to the uttermost that come unto God by him, seeing he ever liveth to make intercession for them. Hebrews 7:25

Thank you God for sending the Way, the Truth and the Life so that I can access the throne of Grace. I know that Jesus stands between me and you to intercede for my highest good. I offer you my praises today Lord, for the sacrifice that Jesus made which rescues my soul from hell, Amen.

OCTOBER 7

The LORD shall preserve thee from all evil: he shall preserve thy soul. Psalm 121:7

Mighty and awesome God, I commit whatever I do today to your care. I thank you for keeping me safe and for granting me success. Help me to honor you with all that I do. In Jesus' name I pray, Amen.

OCTOBER 8

And God shall wipe away all tears from their eyes; and there shall be no more death, neither sorrow, nor crying, neither shall there be any more pain: for the former things are passed away. Revelation 21:4

Lord, I look forward to the time where sickness, pain, sorrow and death are wiped away along with the tears caused by sin. Thank you for a new life and everlasting joy! Amen.

October 9

They that sow in tears shall reap in joy.
Psalm 126:5

Merciful and Loving God, even though I have not had to suffer as some Christians have for their faith, I still cannot express praises enough to thank you for replacing my mourning with gladness. Thank you for the joy that only comes from you, Amen.

October 10

And all things, whatsoever ye shall ask in prayer, believing, ye shall receive. Matthew 21:22

Thank you for the power of prayer God! Please help me to develop a prayer life that affects every part of what I do and is a witness to all I come in contact with. In Jesus' name I pray, Amen.

OCTOBER 11

I will go before thee, and make the crooked places straight: I will break in pieces the gates of brass, and cut in sunder the bars of iron. Isaiah 45:2

You open doors that no man can shut, God. I praise you for a new life that takes me down a completely different path than I was on before. Thank you for revealing your Word to me and calling me to yourself, Amen.

OCTOBER 12

Peace I leave with you, my peace I give unto you: not as the world giveth, give I unto you. Let not your heart be troubled, neither let it be afraid. John 14:27

Lord, you not only came bearing lasting peace, but you died to make it mine. Thank you Lord, for a legacy and a heritage and for a future and a hope in you, Amen.

OCTOBER 13

But in every nation he that feareth him, and worketh righteousness, is accepted with him.
Acts 10:35

Thank you God, for sending Jesus to be condemned so that I could be accepted. Help me to have a fear of displeasing you and to be righteous and holy, acceptable to you. And I ask that you would help our nation be a Godly nation. In your name I pray, Amen.

OCTOBER 14

Have not I commanded thee? Be strong and of a good courage; be not afraid, neither be thou dismayed: for the LORD thy God is with thee whithersoever thou goest.   Joshua 1:9

Lord, whatever affairs I have to attend to and whatever tasks take my attention today, please help me to remember that you are right beside me, helping me, guiding my steps and watching over me. Thank you for your great love, Jesus, Amen.

OCTOBER 15

The liberal soul shall be made fat: and he that watereth shall be watered also himself.
Proverbs 11:25

Mighty and awesome God, you have been so generous with me in so many ways. Help me not to hoard all of the blessings you have poured out so richly. Make me a better giver Lord. Not just to receive your blessing, but to be a blessing to others. Give me an opportunity to give in a special way today, Amen.

OCTOBER 16

Thus saith the LORD, Stand ye in the ways, and see, and ask for the old paths, where is the good way, and walk therein, and ye shall find rest for your souls. But they said, we will not walk therein.
Jeremiah 6:16

The path of Godliness and righteousness has always been your path God. So many people know that you are always there, yet refuse to let you into their hearts. But you are a God of mercy. Reach down to those who need your touch in their lives, Lord. Show them the many opportunities they have to ask forgiveness from you and accept your free gift of salvation. Help me to be your witness today Lord, Amen.

OCTOBER 17

For there is no difference between the Jew and the Greek: for the same Lord over all is rich unto all that call upon him.   Romans 10:12

Lord, your blessings and riches can never be exhausted. It doesn't matter who calls upon your name, you are faithful to answer. Thank you Lord that there is no shame in calling on your name and all who do so will be saved. Teach me to ignore race and color and to share the love of Jesus with a world that needs you, Amen.

OCTOBER 18

But he knoweth the way that I take: when he hath tried me, I shall come forth as gold. Job 23:10

Heavenly Father, you know my heart. Please convict me of anything in my life that is not in line with your will. Help me to come forth as pure gold. In Jesus' name I ask it, Amen.

OCTOBER 19

For in that he himself hath suffered being tempted, he is able to succour them that are tempted. Hebrews 2:18

Lord Jesus, you understand temptation better than anybody. When temptations come, please remind me that you covered all sins on the cross, and you are able to instantly help me when I am tempted to be angry, or act in any way that does not reflect the beauty of Christ. Thank you Lord, that temptations are never too big for us to handle together, Amen.

OCTOBER 20

For the eyes of the Lord are over the righteous, and his ears are open unto their prayers: but the face of the Lord is against them that do evil.   1 Peter 3:12

Righteous God, help me to hold back from deceitful or abusive language, help me to forsake and avoid all evil actions, and help me to seek peace and do all of the good that I can. I know you see it all, Lord.   Please keep your eyes upon me Lord, Amen.

OCTOBER 21

But unto you that fear my name shall the Sun of righteousness arise with healing in his wings; and ye shall go forth, and grow up as calves of the stall. Malachi 4:2

God of Justice, the outcome of your righteous judgment is different for the good and for the evil. I would rather be a frisky calf than a downtrodden person. Help me to be righteous, God, Amen.

OCTOBER 22

If any man serve me, let him follow me; and where I am, there shall also my servant be: if any man serve me, him will my Father honour. John 12:26

God, please help me to serve you with a willing mind. Show me how to be indifferent to the things of this world that are temporary and distract me from my relationship with you so that I can truly follow you. In Jesus' name, Amen.

OCTOBER 23

The LORD also will be a refuge for the oppressed, a refuge in times of trouble.   Psalm 9:9

My God and my Refuge, help me to trust in your Word and stand upon your promises whether in good times or bad. Thank you for being there every minute of every day, Amen.

OCTOBER 24

The blessing of the LORD, it maketh rich, and he addeth no sorrow with it.   Proverbs 10:22

Great and Mighty God, help me to seek out the kind of wealth that you would desire for me. Help me to seek your face with all my heart, Amen.

October 25

And the peace of God, which passeth all under-standing, shall keep your hearts and minds through Christ Jesus.   Philippians 4:7

Thank you God for the awesome quietness of mind that only comes from knowing you. I praise you Lord, for guarding not just my heart, but my mind. I rest in your peace today Jesus, Amen.

October 26

Give thanks unto the LORD, call upon his name, make known his deeds among the people. 1 Chronicles 16:8

Lord I pray that you would be glorified in my praises. I ask that your people would be edified and taught. Lord, may those who don't know you see your glory and be led to call upon your holy name, Amen.

OCTOBER 27

There is none holy as the LORD: for there is none beside thee: neither is there any rock like our God. 1 Samuel 2:2

Thank you Lord, that you are my refuge. There is no other so unchangeably and perfectly holy as you O God. I trust in you today my King and my Rock, Amen.

OCTOBER 28

But speaking the truth in love, may grow up into him in all things, which is the head, even Christ. Ephesians 4:15

Awesome God, help me to have an earnest love of the truth. Teach me as I grow in your Word; guide every part of my life as I mature in the knowledge of you, Amen.

OCTOBER 29

For I know that my redeemer liveth, and that he shall stand at the latter day upon the earth. Job 19:25

Lord, I don't have to convince any other person of my opinions. I don't need to loudly defend myself. I don't need to explain. For me to know that you are on my side is enough. Thank you God, that you are my Defender, Amen.

OCTOBER 30

Then the presidents and princes sought to find occasion against Daniel concerning the kingdom; but they could find none occasion nor fault; forasmuch as he was faithful, neither was there any error or fault found in him.   Daniel 6:4

Heavenly Father, help me to always walk upright in the fear of you with a clean conscience. Let my home, my work, my relationships, and everything else in my life glorify you, Amen.

OCTOBER 31

Knowing this, that the trying of your faith worketh patience.   James 1:3

Jesus, it is because of you that I can be joyful during troubled times. Help me Lord, to strive to be patient when I pray and to know that the answers come in your perfect time. When afflictions come, help me to use them to grow stronger in you. In your name I pray, Amen.

NOVEMBER

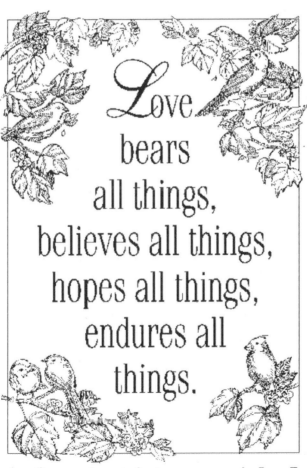

Love bears
all things,
believes all things,
hopes all things,
endures all
things.

1 Corinthians 13:7

November 1

It is good for me that I have been afflicted; that I might learn thy statutes.   Psalm 119:71

Help me to realize Lord, that any type of affliction is an opportunity to gain wholesome discipline and to more highly value the promises and truth in your Word, Amen.

November 2

For our light affliction, which is but for a moment, worketh for us a far more exceeding and eternal weight of glory. 2 Corinthians 4:17

Thank you God, that I can look forward to the awesome reward that you have prepared for your children. Help me not to get bogged down with the troubling things of this world that will soon pass away. In Jesus' name I pray, Amen.

November 3

If ye keep my commandments, ye shall abide in my love; even as I have kept my Father's commandments, and abide in his love.   John 15:10

Heavenly Loving Father, just as you loved Jesus, who was worthy, you love me too, even though I am not. Help me to show my love for you in every area of my life. Help me to love others in the same way that you love me. Amen.

November 4

Bring ye all the tithes into the storehouse, that there may be meat in mine house, and prove me now herewith, saith the LORD of hosts, if I will not open you the windows of heaven, and pour you out a blessing, that there shall not be room enough to receive it. Malachi 3:10

Help me to honor you with all that I have Lord, Amen.

NOVEMBER 5

Ah Lord GOD! behold, thou hast made the heaven and the earth by thy great power and stretched out arm, and there is nothing too hard for thee.   Jeremiah 32:17

Lord God Almighty, you are the fountain of all life and power, there is nothing too difficult for you. Thank you Awesome God for your justice, mercy, and best intention for my life. Whatever situation may arise, I am confident that you are in control. Thank you Jesus, Amen.

NOVEMBER 6

We are troubled on every side, yet not distressed; we are perplexed, but not in despair; Persecuted, but not forsaken; cast down, but not destroyed. 2 Corinthians 4:8-9

God, I can be forsaken by my friends and attacked by my enemies, but you will never ever leave me. Even when there may be internal fear and external turmoil, I am not destroyed. When troubles arise Lord, use them to be glorified in my life, Amen.

November 7

The grass withereth, the flower fadeth: but the word of our God shall stand for ever.   Isaiah 40:8

Lord, all that I have and all that I do are just dry grass and withered flowers! Thank you for your eternal Word. Help me to stand upon its promises today Lord, Amen.

November 8

Salvation belongeth unto the LORD: thy blessing is upon thy people. Selah.   Psalm 3:8

Salvation comes from you O God. No matter what the dangers, you are my salvation. If the trial is in my mind or all around me, I look to you and no other for salvation. Thank you Lord for your grace and mercy and all of the blessings you have lavished upon me, Amen.

November 9

Now the end of the commandment is charity out of a pure heart, and of a good conscience, and of faith unfeigned.   1 Timothy 1:5

Lord please help me to keep my heart and mind pure, my conscience clear, and my faith strong so that nothing can come between me and your grace, Amen.

November 10

But let him ask in faith, nothing wavering. For he that wavereth is like a wave of the sea driven with the wind and tossed.   James 1:6

Heavenly Father, I affirm my confidence in you. Help me not to waver in my faith and to fully trust in your promises. Even when I may not understand why things happen the way they do, help me not to be tossed around as a wave, but to stand steady upon Jesus who is the unmovable Rock, Amen.

NOVEMBER 11

Let us hold fast the profession of our faith without wavering; (for he is faithful that promised) Hebrews 10:23

Thank you Holy God for your faithfulness. Give me opportunities to exercise my faith to make it stronger. I trust in your promises today God. Please help me not to waver, but to draw closer to you, Amen.

NOVEMBER 12

If ye shall ask any thing in my name, I will do it. John 14:14

Guide my asking Lord, that I would desire of you those things you would have me to acquire that are in line with your will. Help me to bless others and to honor you with all that you bless me with. In Jesus' name I ask it, Amen.

NOVEMBER 13

That ye might walk worthy of the Lord unto all pleasing, being fruitful in every good work, and increasing in the knowledge of God;   Colossians 1:10

Gracious Lord, help me to increase my knowledge of you by studying your Word. Give me a stronger desire to know you and to make you known. Help me to be fruitful and to bless others so that they might come to know you also. Help me to be worthy of being called your child and to please you in all that I do, Amen.

NOVEMBER 14

What man is he that feareth the LORD? him shall he teach in the way that he shall choose. Psalm 25:12

Give me a healthy fear of displeasing you Great and Mighty God. Teach me to live a life that totally glorifies you, Amen.

NOVEMBER 15

For if we would judge ourselves, we should not be judged.   1 Corinthians 11:31

Please help me to look after my own affairs Lord, and not to be critical of others. I ask your forgiveness for the many times I have judged other people even though you have forgiven me of so much, Amen.

NOVEMBER 16

Thy word is a lamp unto my feet, and a light unto my path.   Psalm 119:105

Loving and Generous Father, I was born in darkness and stumbled through life until I received your Word. Help me to read and memorize your Word and to always walk in your light. In Jesus' name I pray, Amen.

NOVEMBER 17

The discretion of a man deferreth his anger; and it is his glory to pass over a transgression. Proverbs 19:11

By your grace Heavenly Father, help me to overcome evil with good. Please help me when I get angry so that I will reflect the character of Jesus, Amen.

NOVEMBER 18

And the angel said unto them, Fear not: for, behold, I bring you good tidings of great joy, which shall be to all people.   Luke 2:10

Lord you sent an angel to announce that the way to peace with God and pardon from sin was about to burst out into the world! Thank you Heavenly Father for the joy that comes from being in relationship with you. Thank you God, that because of Jesus, you still banish all fear, Amen.

November 19

Blessed are the pure in heart: for they shall see God.   Matthew 5:8

God, I can make the outside look pure, but that doesn't really matter. You know my heart O God. Only you can cleanse my insides Lord. Help me to have the purity of heart that comes from embracing your mercy and your grace, Amen.

November 20

In the day of my trouble I will call upon thee: for thou wilt answer me. Psalm 86:7

Thank you Heavenly Father that you give and for-give. No matter what other people do, I will put my trust in you. In Jesus' name I praise you today, Amen.

November 21

I am the vine, ye are the branches: He that abideth in me, and I in him, the same bringeth forth much fruit: for without me ye can do nothing. John 15:5

Lord I thank you for being the life giving vine. Denominations and organizations are not your branches, but people are. Just as the branches are nothing without the vine, people are nothing without Jesus. Help us to unite to you through faith in Jesus. In His name I pray, Amen.

November 22

And he said unto him, Well, thou good servant: because thou hast been faithful in a very little, have thou authority over ten cities.   Luke 19:17

Jesus, help me to use the gifts you have given me to their fullest extent. Any gift, talent or ability that I have comes from you. Please show me how I can serve you more as I grow in the knowledge of God, Amen.

November 23

Surely he hath borne our griefs, and carried our sorrows: yet we did esteem him stricken, smitten of God, and afflicted.   Isaiah 53:4

Jesus, my sins were the thorns in your brow, the nails in your hands, and the spear in your side. Thank you for suffering and dying for my sins. I owe you a debt I can never pay back except to love you with all my heart. By your grace I will love and serve you all the days of my life, Amen.

November 24

Wherefore seeing we also are compassed about with so great a cloud of witnesses, let us lay aside every weight, and the sin which doth so easily beset us, and let us run with patience the race that is set before us.   Hebrews 12:1

Holy and Loving Father, sin, any sin, will keep me from doing my best for you. Please help me to throw off anything that slows me down and keeps me from totally serving you. In Jesus' name I pray, Amen.

NOVEMBER 25

Rest in the LORD, and wait patiently for him: fret not thyself because of him who prospereth in his way, because of the man who bringeth wicked devices to pass.   Psalm 37:7

Lord, please help me to not become discontented because of the things I see in the world. The gift of salvation is more righteous, more holy and more profitable than anything the world can give. Thank you God, that I have peace of mind, and a future and a hope that the world does not have. Prosperity on earth is numbered in days, but my happiness with you will last forever.   In Jesus' name I praise you, Amen.

NOVEMBER 26

It is of the LORD's mercies that we are not consumed, because his compassions fail not.
Lamentations 3:22-23

Thank you for your great love and mercy, God. It is only because of your infinite compassion that I am alive to pray this prayer today. Please rest your loving hand upon those who still are searching for answers in life. By your great mercy and compassion lead them to yourself so that they can know your Son Jesus, and be saved by your grace, Amen.

NOVEMBER 27

For whosoever shall call upon the name of the Lord shall be saved.   Romans 10:13

Lord, it doesn't matter where I'm from or what I've done, your promises are true no matter who calls upon your name. Help me to make my life one that is defined by relationship with you. In Jesus' name I pray, Amen.

NOVEMBER 28

They are all gone aside, they are all together become filthy: there is none that doeth good, no, not one.   Psalm 14:3

Lord, whatever is good in any person's life is not of them, but of you. No one can stand on their own right-eousness. Shine through me today Lord so that I reflect the righteousness of Jesus. Let us see the corruption of our own nature and the urgent need for you. In Jesus' name I pray, Amen.

NOVEMBER 29

And I, if I be lifted up from the earth, will draw all men unto me.   John 12:32

Thank you Jesus that you were lifted up, even up to the cross to die in my place. Thank you that you draw all people to yourself, no matter what they've done. Help me to continue to lift you up. Be glorified in my life today. In Jesus' name I pray, Amen.

NOVEMBER 30

And whatsoever ye do, do it heartily, as to the Lord, and not unto men.   Colossians 3:23

Mighty and awesome God, help me to be diligent in whatever task I have. Please remind me that I work for you first, and all others second. By your loving grace and mercy help me to always do my best. In Jesus' name I pray, Amen.

DECEMBER

What is sown is perishable, what is raised is imperishable.

1 Corinthians 15:42

DECEMBER 1

Not forsaking the assembling of ourselves together, as the manner of some is; but exhorting one another: and so much the more, as ye see the day approaching.   Hebrews 10:25

Heavenly Father, help me to see how I can be of more service to my Christian brothers and sisters. Show me ways to stir others into a more abundant life in you, Amen.

DECEMBER 2

Though I walk in the midst of trouble, thou wilt revive me: thou shalt stretch forth thine hand against the wrath of mine enemies, and thy right hand shall save me.   Psalm 138:7

Mighty and Awesome God, I thank you that you are always available to rescue your children so they may be revived by your Holy Spirit. Thank you that you do not forsake those who have been made new in Christ Jesus, Amen.

DECEMBER 3

For whosoever will save his life shall lose it: and whosoever will lose his life for my sake shall find it. Matthew 16:25

Lord by the Grace of God, I renounce the effort of trying to live this temporary life for myself and I give it to you. From now on I want to give you all of the credit and all of the glory. Help me to live a life dedicated to Jesus, not just to avoid hell, but to serve you and have eternal life in Christ, Amen.

DECEMBER 4

For the LORD giveth wisdom: out of his mouth cometh knowledge and understanding.   Proverbs 2:6

Lord, today I acknowledge you as my source of wisdom. Please help me to gain knowledge and understanding from your Holy Word and rightly apply it in my life. In Jesus name I ask it, Amen.

DECEMBER 5

Notwithstanding in this rejoice not, that the spirits are subject unto you; but rather rejoice, because your names are written in heaven.   Luke 10:20

Heavenly Father, the most important thing you have given to me is eternal life. Any power that I may have comes only from you. Please help me to be careful to give you all of the honor, glory and praise, Amen.

DECEMBER 6

O the depth of the riches both of the wisdom and knowledge of God! how unsearchable are his judgments, and his ways past finding out!   Romans 11:33

Lord, may your awesome wisdom and grace bring me to my knees in adoration. Help me to desire you even more and work towards that day when I will see you face to face, Amen.

DECEMBER 7

And he shall stand and feed in the strength of the LORD, in the majesty of the name of the LORD his God; and they shall abide: for now shall he be great unto the ends of the earth.   Micah 5:4

Heavenly Father I thank you for the power, wisdom and stability that come from knowing you. Help me to walk in your love and in your grace.   In Jesus' name I pray, Amen.

DECEMBER 8

Thou hast put gladness in my heart, more than in the time that their corn and their wine increased. Psalm 4:7

Lord, so much more than material possessions, I thank you for the favor you have bestowed upon me as your child. Please help me to release my attraction to temporary prosperity and to be wholly satisfied in you, Amen.

DECEMBER 9

But as for you, ye thought evil against me; but God meant it unto good, to bring to pass, as it is this day, to save much people alive.   Genesis 50:20

Great God, you made Joseph into a greater blessing to his family than he ever could have been without you, Lord. When people say or do things that are meant for my harm, be with me as you were with Joseph and be glorified in the outcome. I put all my trust in you Lord, Amen.

DECEMBER 10

The LORD preserveth all them that love him: but all the wicked will he destroy.   Psalm 145:20

Holy God, you have always been on my side when it comes to trials and temptations. Thank you God that you have victory planned for me and not failure. Please help me to love you even more, Amen.

DECEMBER 11

But ye shall receive power, after that the Holy Ghost is come upon you: and ye shall be witnesses unto me both in Jerusalem, and in all Judaea, and in Samaria, and unto the uttermost part of the earth. Acts 1:8

God of Power, I thank you so much for your power; not human power, but moral and spiritual power. Help me to be a witness of my personal knowledge of you. Be with me today as I share your love with others, Amen.

DECEMBER 12

Jesus Christ the same yesterday, and to day, and for ever.   Hebrews 13:8

Unchangeable God, no one has ever gotten saved without Jesus, and no ever can be. Help me to stay strong in your Word, and follow you the rest of my life, Amen.

DECEMBER 13

The LORD shall preserve thy going out and thy coming in from this time forth, and even for evermore. Psalm 121:8

Heavenly Father, I cannot rely on any man, machine, or idea to protect me. My confidence is in you alone Lord. I will never look to the hills, God, but to you who made the hills. Please help me to trust you even more, Mighty God, Amen.

DECEMBER 14

Yea doubtless, and I count all things but loss for the excellency of the knowledge of Christ Jesus my Lord: for whom I have suffered the loss of all things, and do count them but dung, that I may win Christ, Philippians 3:8

Lord God, you are my Prophet, Priest and King. You teach me wisdom, forgive my sins and live in my heart. Thank you for taking my affections off of the worthless things and garbage that the world has to offer. Please help me to increase my faith and have a stronger desire for more of you, Amen.

DECEMBER 15

Take therefore no thought for the morrow: for the morrow shall take thought for the things of itself. Sufficient unto the day is the evil thereof.
Matthew 6:34

Lord, please help me to not borrow extra trouble from tomorrow when there is enough here today. Rather than anticipating tomorrow, I want to put all of my attention on you today and trust you for my immediate needs. Thank you God that the word "worry" is not part of your vocabulary and there really is no need for it, Amen.

DECEMBER 16

He that believeth on me, as the scripture hath said, out of his belly shall flow rivers of living water.
John 7:38

Lord Jesus, living water comes only from you. Help me to be a fountain of your love, your grace, your compassion and your mercy. In your name I pray, Amen.

DECEMBER 17

Seek good, and not evil, that ye may live: and so the LORD, the God of hosts, shall be with you, as ye have spoken.   Amos 5:14

Heavenly Father, you are always ready to grant blessings to your children. Please help me to put away misery, blame and evil and to embrace repentance and the freedom of forgiveness so I can receive all that you have in store for me, Amen.

DECEMBER 18

Be careful for nothing; but in every thing by prayer and supplication with thanksgiving let your requests be made known unto God.   Philippians 4:6

Lord I release all anxiety and stress today, and give you all of the praise and thanks for every situation in my life. Help me to always come before you with gratitude instead of complaining. In Jesus' name I pray, Amen.

DECEMBER 19

Then Philip opened his mouth, and began at the same scripture, and preached unto him Jesus. Acts 8:35

Great and Mighty God, you sent Philip down a deserted road to tell of how Jesus suffered, died and rose again and how you commanded that your Word be preached so people would repent and be baptized. Wherever you send me Lord, help me to take Jesus with me and be your representative. You were with Philip, Lord. Be with me too, Lord, Amen.

DECEMBER 20

The angel of the LORD encampeth round about them that fear him, and delivereth them.   Psalm 34:7

Thank you God, for sending angels to watch over me and stand with me against the powers of darkness. You never said "seek me in vain". Thank you God, for the power of prayer. Thank you for deliverance, Amen.

DECEMBER 21

Walk in wisdom toward them that are without, redeeming the time. Let your speech be always with grace, seasoned with salt, that ye may know how ye ought to answer every man.   Colossians 4:5-6

Lord, help me to have consideration of everyone, especially those who don't know you. Show me opportunities to do them good. Help me to season my speech with grace to attract and not repel. Help me to say what is right for the moment and to reflect the beauty of Christ, Amen.

DECEMBER 22

And not only so, but we also joy in God through our Lord Jesus Christ, by whom we have now received the atonement.   Romans 5:11

Thank you awesome God that the unrighteousness that flowed from Adam into us, has been swallowed up by the gift of the righteousness of Jesus, given to us by your grace through faith in him. Thank you for covering my sins. Help me to be more like you, Amen.

DECEMBER 23

Teach me, O LORD, the way of thy statutes; and I shall keep it unto the end.   Psalm 119:33

Thank you God of Wisdom, not just for mere words, but for the knowledge in Scripture that I can rightly apply to my life. Thank you for giving me an understanding and a revelation of your Word, Amen.

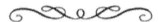

DECEMBER 24

And when he had sent them away, he departed into a mountain to pray.   Mark 6:46

Lord, help me to take time away to be spent alone with you everyday. In Jesus' name, Amen.

DECEMBER 25

And she shall bring forth a son, and thou shalt call his name JESUS: for he shall save his people from their sins.   Matthew 1:21

Lord your name means Savior. Thank you for coming to rescue us from the curse of sin, all who would accept and follow you, Amen.

DECEMBER 26

He will not suffer thy foot to be moved: he that keepeth thee will not slumber.   Psalm 121:3

Thank you for watching over me God. I can rest in confidence of you every minute of every day. In Jesus' name I praise you today, Amen.

DECEMBER 27

When Christ, who is our life, shall appear, then shall ye also appear with him in glory. Colossians 3:4

Thank you Lord, for delivering me out of darkness and into the light. Help me to walk in that light until you return, Amen.

DECEMBER 28

Finally, be ye all of one mind, having compassion one of another, love as brethren, be pitiful, be courteous: 1 Peter 3:8

Lord, help me to rejoice with my brothers and sisters, to sorrow with them, to love them and show them compassion. Help me to treat them as equals and to show loving respect, Amen.

DECEMBER 29

Therefore take no thought, saying, What shall we eat? or, What shall we drink? or, Wherewithal shall we be clothed? (For after all these things do the Gentiles seek:) for your heavenly Father knoweth that ye have need of all these things. But seek ye first the kingdom of God, and his righteousness; and all these things shall be added unto you.   Matthew 6:31-33

Thank you God for helping me to look beyond the present and not worry about things of this life. Help me to make knowing you my priority. Thank you for knowing what I need in advance and blessing me, Amen.

DECEMBER 30

And be not conformed to this world: but be ye transformed by the renewing of your mind, that ye may prove what is that good, and acceptable, and perfect, will of God.   Romans 12:2

Help me each day Lord, to not just outwardly put off the old things of the world, but to renew my mind with a spiritual transformation, giving me pure thoughts and right motives. In Jesus' name I pray, Amen.

DECEMBER 31

And came and preached peace to you which were afar off, and to them that were nigh.
Ephesians 2:17

Thank you Lord, that sinners like me who were such a great distance from you could still access your peace. Thank you God, that I am brought into your presence with acceptance. In Jesus' name I praise you today, Amen.

ANSWERS TO PRAYER